INSIGHTS FOR THE BROKEN

PREPARING FOR THE DAY WHEN LIFE STOPS WORKING AND YOUR FAITH IS TESTED

MIKE WOODRUFF

Christ Church
100 N. Waukegan Road, Lake Forest, IL 60045
847-234-1001 | www.christchurchil.org

Christ Church
100 N Waukegan Rd
Lake Forest, Illinois 60045
847-234-1001
www.christchurchil.org

Scripture quotations noted (NIV) are taken from the HOLY BIBLE, NEW
INTERNATIONAL VERSION®. Copyright 1973, 1978, and 1984 by International
Bible Society Used by permission of Zondervan Bible Publishing House.
All rights reserved.

All Scripture passages are taken from the NIV unless otherwise noted.

Scripture quotations noted KJV are taken from the Holy Bible, King James
Version, Cambridge, 1769.

Scripture quotations noted NASB are taken from the Holy Bible, New
American Standard Version. Copyright 1960, 1962, 1963, 1968, 1977 by The
Lockman Foundation. All rights reserved.

Cover "Flowervase" photograph courtesy of Martin Klimas. Martin Klimas
is a photographer and fine artist, located in Düsseldorf, Germany, and he is
represented in America by the Foley Gallery of New York. For more information
on Martin and his work, please visit www.martin-klimas.de/en/.

START HERE

At least there is hope for a tree:
If it is cut down, it will sprout again,
and its new shoots will not fail.

— JOB—

[INSCRIPTION,
CHAGALL MAQUETTE PAINTING AND TAPESTRY,
REHABILITATION INSTITUTE OF CHICAGO]

During the early days of the first Iraq War, then Secretary of Defense Donald Rumsfeld held court in a White House briefing room. Reports from the field were mostly positive, so Rumsfeld was quite energized and his comments were often entertaining. During one of the briefings he was questioned by Jim Miklaszewski, the NBC Pentagon correspondent, regarding the evidence for weapons of mass destruction in Iraq. Secretary Rumsfeld explained how he and his staff had thought through this matter, noting that they grouped the relevant evidence into three categories.

- First, there were known knowns: that is, things they knew they knew with some certainty;
- Second, there were known unknowns: things they knew with certainty that they did not know;

- Finally, there were unknown unknowns: things they did not know that they did not know.[1]

What follows in this last book of the *Broken* series falls almost exclusively in the first category. However, I want to make a further distinction – one Rumsfeld did not bother with: it's the difference between *knowing in theory* and *knowing first hand*. Few of the insights I share in this book struck me as new. I had known about them before, but the one two punch of my stroke and my father's death brought them home in a new way. Now I knew them personally – i.e. at a deeper, more profound level.

As C.S. Lewis has written, "God whispers to us in our pleasures, speaks in our consciences, but shouts in our pains. It is his megaphone to rouse a deaf world."[2] Trials have a way of driving a point home. They certainly drove home a few for me.

As you're likely aware, this is the fifth book in a series of five. In the first book, *Are You Ready to be Broken?*, I pointed out that trouble eventually knocks on all of our doors, though, as a nation, we're not particularly good at the suffering it brings. I also suggested that the time to prepare for major trials is before they hit, and that if we do, we can emerge stronger and better because of them.

In the second book, *Faith for the Broken*, I noted that our foundational assumptions affect everything, and argued that at least occasionally we need to re-examine them. I went on to note that *real* faith is our first-line of defense against the discouragement that can accompany setbacks and losses.

In the third book, *Big Ideas for the Broken*, I explored those tenets of the Christian faith that I found particularly helpful during my recent struggles: *God is God* (and I am not!); we can be certain that He loves us; we can trust Him; and eternity *changes everything*.

In the fourth book, *Friends for the Broken*, I argued that real friends are both a gift and a further line of defense when things go wrong. I went on to define different levels of relationship, focusing on *Level Four friends* – i.e., those who know you well and whom you can trust completely. I also argued the unequivocal need for these essential friendships and encouraged people to be intentional in cultivating such demanding, risky, but faith-growing friendships.

In this book, *Insights for the Broken*, I am sharing forty personal reflections about suffering. They range from a few sentences to several pages. Consider them like *pensées*,[3] i.e., the somewhat random thoughts of a guy who spent five weeks trapped in a hospital bed.

I started most of these entries while I was attending Day Therapy at Rehabilitation Institute of Chicago (RIC) in Northbrook, Illinois. I've cleaned them up a bit and expanded on a few. Because I didn't know how else to organize them, they are arranged alphabetically.

Finally, because we are heading into Lent, I've added a prayer to make them more devotional. If I had known that this book would roll out during Lent I would have turned them in a very different direction – more about Jesus and less about my struggles!

I hope that you find these insights at least occasionally helpful and appropriately disruptive. Many people have to make every mistake on their own. Some have to make the same mistake multiple times before they learn. (And some seemingly never figure things out no matter how many times they make the same mistake.) But some people can leverage the experiences of others. I hope you are the type that can learn from *my* mistakes so you do not have to go through all of them on your own.

---

[1] Rumsfeld's construction in that news briefing has been widely and hotly debated, and is the source of many follow-up articles, as well as serving as the starting point for a documentary on this former Secretary of Defense [Errol Morris, *The Unknown Known* (History Films, et al., 2013)]. For a good description of the news briefing and the parts played by each participant, see Errol Morris, "The Certainty of Donald Rumsfeld (Part 1)," *The New York Times* (The Opinion Pages), March 25, 2014. A video clip of the statement is available at *YouTube*, and a further extensive article regarding the briefing and the documentary it inspired can be found in David A. Graham, "Rumsfeld's Knowns and Unknowns: The Intellectual History of a Quip," *The Atlantic*, March 27, 2014. The links for the above materials are, respectively, *http://www.defense.*

gov/transcripts/transcript.aspx?transcriptid=2636, http://opinionator. blogs.nytimes.com/2014/03/25/the-certainty-of-donald-rumsfeld-part-1/, https://www.youtube.com/watch?v=GiPe1OiKQuk, and *http:// www.theatlantic.com/politics/archive/2014/03/rumsfelds-knowns-and-unknowns-the-intellectual-history-of-a-quip/359719/.* All online content accessed 2 December 2014.

[2] C.S. Lewis, *The Problem of Pain* (1940; HarperOne, 2001), p. 93.

[3] The allusion is to the similarly disparate but far more profound *Pensées* (Fr., literally "thoughts") by Blaise Pascal, the 17th-century mathematician, philosopher, and religious writer, which similarly consists of jottings of his various ideas, and which, while substantial, remained incomplete at the time of his death in 1662. See for instance Blaise Pascal, *Pensées*, Revised edition, transl. and introduced by A.J. Krailsheimer (Penguin Classics, 1995), or the work directed by Philippe Sellier (Le Livre de Poche, 2000, in French).

AMAZED

We are perishing for lack of wonder, not for lack of wonders.
— G.K. CHESTERTON —

The wonder in our life should always point the greater wonder of the Father.
— HARRY NEAL —

I've been amazed quite a bit lately. For starters, I am amazed both by what neurologists know and by what they do not.

Them: Mr. Woodruff, are you having any other problems besides balance, eyesight, and your voice?

Me: Not really. Nothing worth mentioning.

Them: Everything is worth mentioning. Is there anything else going on that is unusual?

Me: Well, there is one thing, but I doubt it's worth noting.

Them: What is it? We want to know everything.

Me: I don't like my right leg.

Them: Tell us more.

Me: I don't like it. It bothers me. I don't like the way it feels. I especially don't like the way it feels when it gets wet, which makes showers a bit unpleasant.

Them: That sounds like *dysesthesia*.[1]

Me: I think it sounds like I'm crazy. Who doesn't like their right leg?

Them: You're not crazy. Patients who suffer the kind of injury you have report things like this all the time. We can treat that.

Me: How?

Them: We are going to prescribe amitriptyline.

Me: How does amitriptyline work?

Them: We don't know, but it does.

As I said, I'm amazed at what they know and amazed at what they don't know. I'm amazed that they have a word for me not liking my right leg and I'm amazed that they have a treatment for it and amazed that they do not know why the treatment works.

I'm amazed by other things as well.[2] For instance, I'm amazed by how quickly life can fall apart, by how hard it is to balance when you have to think about it, and by just how bad daytime TV is. But lately two things have stood out for their "amazingness." First, I'm amazed by how many hurting people I now see. (I'm sure they were always there, walking around in plain sight. But I didn't see them before. Not like I do now).

Second, I'm amazed by swallowing. Like balance, swallowing fits into the category of profoundly wonderful, complicated, and necessary things that God has taken care of so completely that we do not think about them until they stop working.

During most of the week I spent in neuro-ICU, I was unable to swallow. In fact, one of the first really troubling moments I had came when a neurologist told me that it might be months before I could swallow again. I must have looked horrified when he said this, because he quickly added that if I failed the swallow test – which he was pretty sure was going to happen – they'd schedule me for surgery to insert a port right into my stomach. "That way you'll get all the nutrition you need." In other words, "Don't worry. We're not going to let you starve."

Not swallow for months? Surgery? A port in my stomach? Somehow I didn't feel very encouraged.

The swallow test is also called the *barium test*, and sometimes called the *cookie test*, because if you swallow things like a barium-coated banana and barium-infused pudding, they let you try a bite of a barium-coated cookie.[3]

Anyway, after learning that the swallow test was scheduled for the next day I grew a bit anxious. In fact, I became more anxious about passing the swallow test than I had been about passing any exam since my physics final, sophomore year in college.

As it turned out, I needn't have worried. Much to everyone's surprise, I passed.

I'm not entirely sure how. It just worked. To me it was a God-thing, because in order to swallow properly, *a half dozen different parts of your mouth and throat have to perform a perfectly choreographed dance,* and if any one of them misses a step, down go the dancers – your bite of banana goes down your windpipe instead of your esophagus, and you start to choke.

I briefly tried "studying" for the swallow test, going so far as to ask my ICU nurse for help. But I gave up after listening to her explain how many things had to work in harmony. I decided my time was better spent praying, reasoning that if God didn't turn my ability to swallow back on, I was going to have a port surgically placed in my side.

Thankfully God was gracious to me. I didn't exactly ace the exam, but I did well enough to be cleared for nectar-thick liquids provided I turned my head all the way to the left every time I swallowed, and swallowed twice with each bite, just to be sure I cleared my throat.

Swallowing is amazing.

I was thinking about swallowing (and other things) when I posted the following on my blog on May 6th:

> The more I learn about anything – e.g., the human brain, swallowing – the more amazing I realize God is. He is more brilliant, more beautiful, and more wonderful than we can imagine, and understanding how my body works and watching it recover is a great reminder of that.

It is unthinkable to me that something as complicated as swallowing – an activity that depends on the perfectly choreographed actions of a variety of parts of the mouth and throat – could be the result of blind chance.[4]

I have faith, but not that much.

My experiences with the design – and with a (thankfully) temporary design failure – leads me to believe in an amazing Designer.

The more we study anything, the more we realize how amazing He is.

When does God amaze you?

Consider: Psalm 8; Job 26:8-14

Prayer for the Week – St. Anselm

> *O Lord my God, teach my heart this day where and how to see you; where and how to find you. You have made me and remade me, and you have bestowed on me all the good things I possess. And still I do not know you. I have not yet done that for which I was made. Teach me to seek you, for I cannot seek you unless you teach me, or find you unless you show yourself to me. Let me seek you in my desire; let me desire you in my seeking. Let me find you by loving you; let me love you when I find you.*

---

[1] *Dysethesia*, which is also called *allodynia*, refers to a condition when normal, non-painful stimuli can be misinterpreted by the nervous system as a painful and unpleasant.

[2] "If you think about it, we get robbed of the mystery of being alive. I think we get robbed of the glory of it because we don't remember how we got here. When you get born, you wake up slowly to everything. From birth to 26, God is slowly turning on the lights, and you are groggy and pointing at things, and say "Circle," and, "Blue,", and, "Car," and, "Sex," and then, "Job," and, "Healthcare". The experience is so slow, you could easily come to believe life isn't that big of a deal, that life isn't staggering. Life IS staggering, and we are just too used to it." Donald Miller, *A Million Miles in a Thousand Years: What I Learned While Editing My Life*,

[3] Though no one said as much, I suspect it's also called the *glow-in-the-dark test*, because after that much barium you not only set off Geiger counters, you radiated a yellow-green hue.

[4] According to Evolution 101, aspects of the throats of my ancient ancestors changed as the result of random mutations, and those changes gave said ancestor an evolutionary advantage over his neighbors. Given that most mutations can be harmful – think Down's Syndrome or Tay Sachs disease – there would have likely been many harmful mutations before we got the necessary ones together that were helpful. That is, somehow a *series* of mutations affecting the genes that underlie the functions of the mouth and throat would have to have occurred at exactly the right time and in the right way for our food to only go down one chute (and air, only the other). The complexity of this simple function alone is staggering. The idea that all of this occurred by chance seems astronomical to me.

ANGER

I have no better remedy than anger. If I want to write,
pray, preach well, then I must be angry. Then my entire
blood supply refreshes itself, my mind is made keen,
and all temptations depart.

— MARTIN LUTHER —

Anybody can become angry — that is easy,
but to be angry with the right person and to the right degree
and at the right time and for the right purpose,
and in the right way — that is not within everybody's
power and is not easy.

— ARISTOTLE —

One of the common responses to a major setback is anger.
It generally comes third. After a jarring loss we cycle through
shock, sorrow and struggle. Or, to frame things according
to the way we feel: first we are numb, then we are sad, and
then we get mad.[1]

Although many avoid expressing their anger to God, the
Bible invites us to do so. In fact, it gives us specific prayers to
pray when we are ticked off. For instance, Psalm 69. Eugene
Peterson's paraphrase of it reads this way:

Don't look the other way [God]; your servant can't take it.
I'm in trouble. Answer right now!

Come close, God; get me out of here.
Rescue me from this deathtrap.

You know how they kick me around—
Pin on me the donkey's ears, the dunce's cap.

I'm broken by their taunts,
Flat on my face, reduced to a nothing.

I looked in vain for one friendly face. Not one.
I couldn't find one shoulder to cry on.

They put poison in my soup,
Vinegar in my drink.

Let their supper be bait in a trap that snaps shut;
May their best friends be trappers who'll skin them alive.

Make them become blind as bats,
Give them the shakes from morning to night.

Let them know what you think of them,
Blast them with your red-hot anger.

Burn down their houses,
Leave them desolate with nobody at home.
(Psalm 69:17-25, The Message)

Clearly, those who think "the Bible is full of nice statements
by nice people about how to be really, really nice" haven't
read Psalm 69. Or Psalm 109. Or any of the other

imprecatory psalms.[2] To be fair, most of the "angry psalms" end on an upbeat or conciliatory note. People often feel better after they vent, especially if they also take the time to remind themselves of God's nature and care.

But I am getting ahead of myself. My point is: God does not censor our wails of anguish or our cries of rage. Apparently He is more comfortable with our anger than we are.

And this includes anger directed at him. Indeed, the Bible not only gives us prayers to pray when we are mad at other people, it gives us prayers to pray when we are mad at God.[3]

I know this is surprising to some of you. For starters there is the misperception I mentioned above – i.e., that the Bible is full of nice statements made by nice people. There is also common sense. It's prudent to pick fights wisely. Talking smack with God seems risky.

For years I avoided conflict of all types, especially with God. But Sheri, a few counselors, and the Psalms eventually persuaded me that there was a better way. I came to understand that those who "stuff their grief" stay stuck, while their anger finds an alternate outlet.

This is not to suggest that we are free to vent anywhere and at any time about anything. The biblical writers know better. Through stories, Proverbs, discourse and examples, they provide helpful counsel about anger. Here are some of the things that have jumped out at me in recent days.

- Some people blame everyone else for the things they are angry about, when it's clear to any objective party that the one who is doing the blaming is most at fault.

- Some people's anger never seems to burn out. Among those I saw during my recovery are those who were angry with the nurses, angry with the doctors, or angry about the food. They complained about their spouse or their kids, either because they did not visit, or because they visited too often.

- Sometimes, anger is the appropriate response. It is OK to be angry at sin. In fact, anger is not only occasionally the right response, there is something seriously wrong with a person who cannot get angry.

- But anger is not always justified, even when we think it is. (Anger feels like the right response even when it's not.) And even when it's the right response, it tends to splash outside its banks. As Aristotle said, it's very hard to be angry at the right person for the right reason, in the right way, and for the right period of time.

- Even when anger is justified, it's still dangerous. Although anger is a God-given emotion that can be directed to accomplish good, few of us are able to be angry and act wisely. This must be why the Apostle Paul offers specific counsel to those who are growing agitated. "In your anger do not sin. Do not let the sun go down while you are still angry, and do not give the devil a foothold." (Ephesians 4:26f)

- We often take things out on others when our struggles are actually with God. Some do not see this. Jacob didn't. If you had asked him to name his chief adversary he would have said Esau. Only later did it become clear to him that his problems were with God (and himself).

- It is OK to be angry at God, but it's not a good idea to stay that way. We need to bring our complaints to him and work things out.[4] The ancient Hebrews often expressed their frustrations with God to each other. That did not work out well for them. Moses and David, among others, expressed their frustrations directly to God. That works.

- Being angry at God is preferable to being apathetic. God can handle our anger. His shoulders are broad enough. In fact, taking our anger to him is a form of worship. We should not be afraid to plead our case. We should wrestle with God in prayer more often.[5]

Do you have an anger problem? Who are you angry with? Are you able to be angry and yet not sin?

Do you have the courage to address your anger with God?

Consider: Psalm 109; Ephesians 4:26-5:2

Prayer for the Week – St. Anselm

> *O Lord my God, teach my heart this day where and how to see you; where and how to find you. You have made me and remade me, and you have bestowed on me all the good things I possess. And still I do not know you. I have not yet done that for which I was made. Teach me to seek you, for I cannot seek you unless you teach me, or find you unless you show yourself to me. Let me seek you in my desire; let me desire you in my seeking. Let me find you by loving you; let me love you when I find you.*

---

[1] In the sermon series I noted that three additional – optional – stages follow: surrender, sanctification and service.

[2] The psalms that contain anger, invoke judgment, or call down curses are referred to as imprecatory psalms. The verb "imprecate" means "to pray evil against" or "to invoke a curse upon, " thus imprecatory Psalms are called such because they contain a particularly vigorous attitude toward an enemy.

[3] There are a subset of psalms where the anger is directed at God. The template for the development of the psalm, in most of these, is *orientation*, then *disorientation*, and then *re-orientation*. Or, said another way, *this is what is going on*, then *this is how I feel about it*, and *now that I've vented, I see it another way*. Psalm 69 – the opening lines of which are quoted above – follows this pattern.

[4] Rick Warren argues that Jacob's prayer follows the pattern of many laments, which he gives the acronym of CARE. First Jacob *complains*, and then he *appeals*. He then *reminds* God of what He has said. And then, he *expresses* trust in God. Warren argues that this is the pattern that David, Job, Jacob, and Habakkuk all followed. See for instance Job 13:15 and Habakkuk 3:17-19. See Doug Humphreys, "Praying When Life Does Not Make Sense," in *Next Steps*, Creekside Covenant Church, Nov. 19, 2013, at *http://ecreekside.com/praying-when-life-does-not-make-sense*, accessed 2 December 2014.

[5] Jesus wrestles with God in prayer in the Garden of Gethsemane, see Matthew 26:36f.

ANSWERS

Praise be to the God and Father of our Lord Jesus Christ,
the Father of compassion and the God of all comfort,
who comforts us in all our troubles, so that we
can comfort those in any trouble with the comfort
we ourselves receive from God.

— THE APOSTLE PAUL —

When I lay these questions before God I get no answer.
But a rather special sort of 'No answer.' It is not the locked
door. It is more like a silent, certainly not uncompassionate,
gaze. As though He shook His head not in refusal but waiving
the question. Like, 'Peace, child; you don't understand.

— C.S. LEWIS —

When we are suffering what do we need most? Relief? Encouragement? An explanation as to why?

In *How Long O Lord?*, a book about suffering, prolific author and distinguished professor Dr. D. A. Carson writes:

> God is less interested in answering our questions than in other things: securing our allegiance, establishing our faith, nurturing a desire for holiness… God tells us a great deal about Himself; but the mysteries that remain

are not going to be answered at a merely theoretical and intellectual level... Ultimately, the Christian will take refuge from questions about God not in proud, omniscient explanations but in adoring worship.[1]

I like to ask questions as much as the next guy, but as I've noted already, other than wanting to learn enough to ensure that I avoid a second stroke, I've not been very interested in knowing why I had the first one – i.e., "why did God allow this to happen to me?"

My decision not to question God is not the result of any piety. It's just clear to me that knowing why it happened would not bring any of the real comfort that Paul speaks of above (in 2 Corinthians 1.3f). What I want most is God, not answers.

What are you really seeking when you ask God, "Why?"

Consider: Habakkuk 1:1-11; 2 Corinthians 1

Prayer for the Week – St. Anselm

> *O Lord my God, teach my heart this day where and how to see you; where and how to find you. You have made me and remade me, and you have bestowed on me all the good things I possess. And still I do not know you. I have not yet done that for which I was made. Teach me to seek you, for I cannot seek you unless you teach me, or find you unless you show yourself to me. Let me seek you in my desire; let me desire you in my seeking. Let me find you by loving you; let me love you when I find you.*

------

[1] D. A. Carson, *How Long, O Lord?: Reflections on Suffering and Evil*, 2nd edn., (Baker Academic, 2006), p. 219.

ANXIETY

Anxiety does not empty tomorrow of its sorrows,
but only empties today of its strength.

Do not be anxious about anything, but in every situation,
by prayer and petition, with thanksgiving,
present your requests to God. And the peace of God,
which transcends all understanding, will guard
your hearts and your minds in Christ Jesus.

When I worked as a management consultant we frequently referred to the following equation:

$$A1 > A2 = No\ Change$$

Translated it means: when the anxiety associated with changing (A1) is greater than the anxiety associated with not changing (A2), change will not occur. In other words, if the hassles involved in learning a new software program eclipse the fear of not learning it (e.g., being let go), you do not learn the new system.

I first ran across this equation while facilitating a team that was working to restructure the labor force of an oil refinery. There was a lot of resistance to this project. So much that after we finished some on the team favored soft-selling our proposed changes, arguing that this would lower people's resistance and make acceptance more likely. Others – and I was in this second camp – argued that we needed to be honest about the challenges of changing, but also clear about the risks of not changing.

What we all agreed upon was that if A1 remained greater than A2, nothing would happen.

Some think Paul's counsel to the Philippians (quoted above) demands that we avoid anxiety at all cost. That is not true. Paul said some anxiety producing things himself. So did Jesus. Take Christ's words in Matthew 10:28.

> Do not be afraid of those who kill the body but cannot kill the soul. Rather, be afraid of the One (i.e., God) who can destroy both soul and body in hell.

That is an anxiety producing statement if ever there was one.

You might argue that there are subtle differences between anxiety, fear and worry. But that is an exercise in missing the point: while some things are not worth worrying about, others are.

The good life requires us to order our heart – and that means learning to love some things and avoid (even hate or fear) others.

For what it's worth, the A1 > A2 equation served me well in rehabilitation. There were times when my therapists asked me to do things that I did not want to do, often because I knew that if I tried I'd stumble around, crash into a few things and perhaps get nauseous. At the very least I would look like an uncoordinated fool, again.

But my fear of what would happen if I didn't get better (A2) was so high that I was always motivated to at least try.

Some believe that life would be better if we avoided all anxiety. This is not possible. Sometimes we have to stare down the things that hold us back.

Is there a positive change you are too anxious to make?

Consider: Philippians 4:6-8; Romans 8:28-30

Prayer for the Week – St. Anselm

> *O Lord my God, teach my heart this day where and how to see you; where and how to find you. You have made me and remade me, and you have bestowed on me all the good things I possess. And still I do not know you. I have not yet done that for which I was made. Teach me to seek you, for I cannot seek you unless you teach me, or find you unless you show yourself to me. Let me seek you in my desire; let me desire you in my seeking. Let me find you by loving you; let me love you when I find you.*

ASSUMPTIONS

Your assumptions are your windows on the world.
Scrub them off every once in a while,
or the light won't come in.

— ISAAC ASIMOV —

Any faith that does not command the one who holds it
is not a real belief; it is a pseudo belief only.
And it might shock some of us profoundly
if we were brought suddenly face to face with our beliefs
and forced to test them in the fires of practical living.

— A.W. TOZER —

I started working on *Broken* well before I had my stroke.
I remember the exact moment I decided that a series on
suffering was needed. It was as I walked out of the hospital
room of Robert (not his real name) after he had suffered his
third heart attack.

Robert was in his early 80s, had made lots of money, lived in
a big houses, had many nice cars and – from what I could tell
– had not denied himself many things, think: lots of alcohol,
lots of women and lots of travel.

He had 'lived large' until a health scare in his mid-70s led to some reflective moments. It was around that time that he started showing up at Christ Church, made a profession of faith, and started heading down a different path.

I had some concerns about Robert's faith, mostly because he tended to wield it like a knight wields a battleax. On more than one occasion he'd taken some swings at me. To be honest, time with him usually left me conflicted. On the one hand, I appreciated how fearlessly he talked about Jesus; on the other, I kept waiting to see a little of Christ's demeanor manifest itself in his life. Sometimes Robert made me smile, but just as often he made me wince.

In an effort to encourage him to grow in Christ-likeness, I invited Robert into a Bible Study I was leading. During these weekly sessions I saw some positive signs: Robert was quick to admit that he was often a jerk and that he had a lot to learn. But our last conversation was not encouraging. It happened at the hospital.

Robert had just suffered his third heart-attack, and though it was minor, the doctors had made it clear that he wouldn't survive the next one. When I stopped by to visit him he came out swinging. As far as he was concerned, both God and I had let him down. I assured Robert that God's promises were true, laughed off his comments about me and – because he had guests – said I'd stop by the next day so we could talk more. As I walked out of the room I thought: I've let Robert down. He is surprised that he is suffering. Like so many others he thought that if he placed his faith in God his problems would go away. The equation looked like this: Belief = Blessing. That is, belief in God equals a blessing from God, and a "blessing from God" means "no problems." Certainly, no heart attacks.

I decided that when I saw him next I'd let him vent, ask him to explain the basics of the Christian faith to me, and then take it from there.

But that conversation never happened. Robert died an hour after I walked out of his room.

I was shaken by Robert's death – or, to be more specific, I was shaken by the fact that I had walked out of his room rather than push him for clarity about life, God and the Gospel.

Robert is a big reason that I decided to write *Broken*. There are a lot of Roberts out there. That is, there are lots who have signed up for: Belief = Blessing.

Of course there is some truth to this equation. Belief in Christ does lead to blessings, but we need to qualify both belief and blessings.[1]

As with other efforts to simplify things, it doesn't always

work. Nevertheless, it can be helpful to reduce your thinking down to a simple formula. Here are a few:

- Karma: Good person x Good life = Good Results[2]
- The American Dream: Hard work = having more than your parents
- The Gospel: Bad Person x Saving Faith = Justification and later Glorification

What equation do you subscribe to? Does it have room for suffering, or are you a Robert?

What do you believe "believing in God" is really about?

Consider: John 16:25-33; 1 Peter 5:6-11

Prayer for the Week – Mother Teresa

Dear Jesus, help me to spread thy fragrance everywhere I go. Flood my soul with Thy spirit and love. Penetrate and possess my whole being so utterly that all my life may only be a radiance of Thine. Shine through me and be so in me that every soul I come in contact with may feel Thy presence in my soul. Let them look up and see no longer me but only Jesus. Stay with me and then I shall begin to shine as you shine, so to shine as to be a light to others.

<hr/>

[1] Believing in God is not enough, for as James says, "Faith without works is dead." Yes, we are saved by faith alone in Christ alone, but true faith manifests itself in a changed life. Furthermore, the blessings we receive may or may not happen this side of the grave. And for that matter, they may or may not be easily recognized as a blessing. (In some ways my stroke was a horrible thing. In other ways it was a conduit to many wonderful things.)

[2] To be fair, this also sounds a bit like the Book of Proverbs

ATTITUDE

People are about as happy as they make up their mind to be.
— ABRAHAM LINCOLN —

Attitude is a little thing that makes a big difference.
— WINSTON CHURCHILL —

———————————————

How much depends on our attitude? How much of an advantage do the 'half-fulls' have over the 'half-empties'? A lot? None?

Some – think football coaches, sales-trainers, TV preachers and the people who write the books they sell at airport kiosks – imply that attitude changes just about everything. They assure us that "It's not the size of the dog in the fight, but the size of the fight in the dog." All we need to do is think positively and we can 'Turn lemons into lemonade' and 'scars into stars.' After all, 'we are victors not victims.'

Are they right?

I started thinking about attitudes generally – and my attitude in particular – shortly after an intake interview with the RIC staff psychologist. In response to my surprise at being asked to meet with a psychologist he told me that many stroke victims become depressed. I later learned that some estimate the number to be as high as eighty percent.

Eighty percent! Eighty percent of stroke victims become depressed. My first thought was that that statistic alone probably pushed more than a few over the edge.

I'd actually wondered about the impact of attitude long before that moment. In fact, among my sermon files is one labeled "attitudes" and another labeled "positive thinking." The latter is not so much a collection of positive thoughts as it is a collection of articles critiquing positive thinking – e.g., "Positively Wrong" and "Negative Thoughts About Positive Thinking."[1]

After spending a few hours sifting through these files – thinking about thinking generally and positive thinking in particular – I am left with a few thoughts.

First, we need to define our terms. I think that of the reasons this topic is both confusing and a bit controversial is because there is so little agreement as to what we are talking about – attitude? resilience? faith? emotions? persistence? All of the above?

For that matter, there is little agreement about what a "can-do" attitude can do: keep people from quitting? Make people happy? Guarantee a win?

Second, Tigger trumps Eeyore. If I'm taking a trip, fielding a team or starting a project, I'd prefer to populate it with can-dos over can-nots any day. Why? Because those who think they can and those who think they cannot are often both right, therefore I want the cans. A positive attitude does help.

Third, if you are leading a team and you are forced to pick between someone with a negative attitude and someone infected with the Ebola virus, take the person with the virus. I say this for three reasons.

- **Negative thoughts weigh more.** It takes more than one positive thought to make up for a negative one. Some say it takes ten. So unless you have hundreds of positive comments lying around, avoid those who ooze despair.

- **Negative thoughts are contagious.** Negativity spreads like cancer. It goes viral faster than a Taylor Swift video.

- **Negative thinking doesn't lead anywhere.** During my stay at RIC I not only did everything they asked me to, I signed up for everything they offered – including crafts class where – for the first time since 3rd grade – I strung beads and painted pottery. My thinking was, "if they think this will help me get better I am going to try it." After all, when I sat in my room I could easily feel sorry for myself and pout. And I was sure that pouting was not going to get me anywhere. I could either work to improve or accept my current status. Being positive might not work, but being negative was sure not to.[2]

Fourth, we need to be pushed. Those who challenge us to 'dig deeper' and 'push harder' almost always do us a favor, because left on our own we settle. Whether it's a track coach, a sales manager or a piano teacher, we run faster, try harder and improve more rapidly when we are pushed by someone who believes in us.

Fifth, it's easy to slip into a death spiral and hard to get out of one. This past week I met with two men who were dangerously close to losing hope. Both were capable and accomplished. They had closed deals, won awards, climbed the ladder and made lots of money. But now they were – to quote a friend from Alabama – "lower than a snakes belly in a tire rut." What had gone wrong? They had both suffered back-to-back failures. That is all it took. They now doubted that the sun would come up tomorrow morning.

I've seen this before. When our life is working things look like this:

But when something goes wrong the whole equation if flipped upside down.

When someone falls into this type of death spiral they typically need help getting out of it. Solomon said as much in Ecclesiastes 4:

> Two are better than one,
>> because they have a good return for their labor:
> If either of them falls down,
>> one can help the other up.

Sixth, most "Yes You Cans" overstate their case. So far I've said, pick *yes* over *no, Tigger* over *Eeyore* and *half-full* over *half-empty*. I now offer this caution: be careful of the Apostles of Positive, because they almost always overstate their case. They start out talking about hard work and good choices but then slip into nonsense about positive energy fields and the ability of our thoughts to alter reality. Sometimes they want you to walk on hot coals. If you listen carefully you can usually hear the music from the Twilight Zone playing in the background.

Those of you who read book two may remember seeing this before. Those who drink too much of the Positive Attitude Punch ascribe the same attributes to positive thinking that some people mistakenly ascribe to faith – i.e., they believe in the power of their belief. Let me remind you, that is not the way things work. As I noted back in Book Two, *Faith for the Broken*, though you may believe that a rickety, old bridge will support you, your ability to cross the bridge is only as viable as the bridge. Believing that it will hold up doesn't make it stronger. Our faith is only ever as good as the object in which we invest it.

So Why Does Yes Work?

Exactly why do can-dos trump can-nots? It turns out that it's not that great of a mystery. In fact, if we listen carefully to those who make "yes" work, we hear them celebrate one (or more) of the following three things: preparation, perseverance or perspective.

Preparation: It turns out that the "Yes I cans" work harder. As a football player, Roger Staubach led the Dallas Cowboys to five Super Bowl appearances. As a businessman he built a multi-billion dollar real estate firm. Those looking on from a distance often comment on his calm confidence. Is this positive attitude what lifts him above others? Perhaps it helps, but if you listen to Staubach, he attributes his success to hard work. "It takes a lot of unspectacular preparation to get spectacular results."

Seasoned leaders have confidence in something other than confidence itself. Their positive attitude may inspire the confidence of others, but their confidence does not lie in their confidence. It rests in a good plan or diligent preparation.

Perseverance: A second way a positive attitude helps people succeed is that it keeps them from quitting. This was part of Churchill's brilliance. He kept people from quitting when others thought there was no hope. He said as much. In his famous speech to the students at Harrow School he said simply, "Never give in, never give in, never, never, never, never—in nothing, great or small, large or petty—never give in except to convictions of honor and good sense."[3]

Perspective: Finally, one of the other reasons some keep trying – and succeed – long after others have retreated or quit, is because they see things differently. Two biblical examples should suffice. David's victory over Goliath was inspired by faith in a great God. But might it also be that David saw things differently. While others saw Goliath as too big to fight, David appears to have viewed him as too big of a target to miss. He famously refused Saul's armor in favor of a very different approach.

Secondly, there is the Apostle's Paul's reference to himself in his letter to the Ephesians. Though he wrote this letter while a prisoner in Rome, he does not describe himself as a prisoner in chains, but an ambassador in chains.

Several months of rehabilitation has made it clear to me that the way we think about things matters a great deal. A positive attitude may not be able to instantly restore the lack of balance of a stroke patient, but the positive attitude of a therapist or a nurse just might keep that patient working on their balance exercises long enough that they can stand on their own.

Our attitude doesn't change the facts on the ground, but it can keep us focused on what we need to be doing.

Half-full really does win.

How does your attitude impact those around you?

Consider: Ecclesiastes 4:8-12; James 1:2-5

Prayer for the Week – Mother Teresa

> *Dear Jesus, help me to spread thy fragrance everywhere I go. Flood my soul with Thy spirit and love. Penetrate and possess my whole being so utterly that all my life may only be a radiance of Thine. Shine through me and be so in me that every soul I come in contact with may feel Thy presence in my soul. Let them look up and see no longer me but only Jesus. Stay with me and then I shall begin to shine as you shine, so to shine as to be a light to others.*

[1] My favorite comment among them is the suggestion that while the Apostle Paul is appealing, Peale (i.e., Normal Vincent Peale, a well-known champion of positive thinking) was appalling.

[2] By the way, I suspect that having a positive attitude was part of the job description for the doctors, nurses and therapists at RIC. They celebrated the smallest achievements and cheered on the smallest of efforts. Some of the time I thought it was too much – they would tell me I was doing well when I thought otherwise – but the more I watched them interact with others the more I saw the importance of the encouragement they offered.

[3] There is quite a bit of myth surrounding this speech. Though it was short, it was longer than some claim. (Many suggest that the entire speech was "Never give in. Never give in. Never, never, never, never give in." It was actually two pages long. But the essence of his speech – and one of the brilliant aspects of his leadership – was his indefatigable spirit.

AVOIDANCE

If there's one thing I learned in Al-Anon,
it's that you got to face the music
because it just grows louder when you ignore it.

— VICKI COVINGTON —

For I am about to fall, and my pain is ever with me…
LORD, do not forsake me; do not be far from me, my God.
Come quickly to help me, my Lord and my Savior.

— PSALM 27: 17, 21 —

Some try to avoid pain, especially emotional pain. Others try to ignore it. Neither approach works.

In Jerry Sittser's book, *A Grace Disguised*, he tells the heartbreaking story of losing his mother, wife and youngest daughter in an automobile accident. The grief he experienced was terrible and his faith hung in tatters.

Sittser, a Christian counselor, wondered how he could continue to counsel others when he needed so much help himself. But his life turned around after he had a kind of "waking dream" in which he chased the sun as it was sinking over the horizon. He was running westward to catch it, but he failed and the darkness swallowed him up.

When he shared his dream with his sister she told him that the only way to catch the sun would be to turn around and run east until he met the sunrise. Sittser writes:

> I discovered in that moment that I had the power to choose the direction my life would head …. I decided from that point on to walk into the darkness rather than try to outrun it, to let my experience of loss take me on a journey wherever it would lead, and to allow myself to be transformed by my suffering rather than to think I could somehow avoid it.[1]

Some try to avoid or ignore pain, especially emotional pain. It does not work.

Where have you experienced "helpful" pain in your life?

Consider: Joshua 1:6-9; Proverbs 3:5-6

Prayer for the Week – Mother Teresa

> *Dear Jesus, help me to spread thy fragrance everywhere I go. Flood my soul with Thy spirit and love. Penetrate and possess my whole being so utterly that all my life may only be a radiance of Thine. Shine through me and be so in me that every soul I come in contact with may feel Thy presence in my soul. Let them look up and see no longer me but only Jesus. Stay with me and then I shall begin to shine as you shine, so to shine as to be a light to others.*

[1] Jerry Sittser, *A Grace Disguised*: *How the Soul Grows Through Loss* (Zondervan, 2005), p. 42.

BROKEN

Come to me, all you who are weary and burdened,
and I will give you rest.
Take my yoke upon you and learn from me,
for I am gentle and humble in heart,
and you will find rest for your souls.
For my yoke is easy and my burden is light.

— JESUS, THE GOSPEL OF MATTHEW —

While Jesus was having dinner at Levi's house,
many tax collectors and sinners were eating with him and
his disciples, for there were many who followed him.
When the teachers of the law who were Pharisees
saw him eating with the sinners and tax collectors,
they asked his disciples: "Why does he eat
with tax collectors and sinners?"
On hearing this, Jesus said to them,
"It is not the healthy who need a doctor, but the sick.
I have not come to call the righteous, but sinners."

— THE GOSPEL OF MARK —

Not quite three months after my stroke, I spoke at our
weekend services at Christ Church. I was not ready to return

to pastoring, but when a guest speaker cancelled, I decided that it would be good for me to "show up broken."

When I say "broken" I mean weak and vulnerable. I couldn't stand, my voice was whisper-thin and my vision was awful. But I saw this as an opportunity to do several things: to thank people for their prayers; to share some of what I was learning; and most of all, to model the behavior I wanted others to follow – i.e., you show up at church even when life isn't working.

Our tendency is to hide when we are hurt – either by staying away altogether, or by putting on our game-face and acting like we are doing OK when we are not. I wanted to show up when it was obvious that I was not OK.

Lest you think I acted bravely, let me note that there is little shame associated with having a vertebral brain dissection. People aren't mad at me. I did not do anything wrong – there is no moral failure involved. If anything, they feel sorry for me. Would I have shown up if I'd been caught stealing church funds, violating my marriage vows, lying to the elders or being full of pride? I hope so but I'm not sure. [1]

Many are way ahead of me on this. When they get jostled by life they run to church, either because they believe Jesus' chapter-opening words cited above (Matthew 11:28-30) and are desperate for God (and do not care who knows); or because they expect the church to be a lot more like an

AA meeting – i.e., a place where everyone admits to being broken so, those who stumble in are not judged, they are embraced.

Tragically, many churches are not that way. They talk about AA meeting-levels of grace, but their weekly gatherings are more like high-end health clubs where you can only show up if you are already in great shape. (And where you need to tuck in your shirt, suck in your gut, and comb your hair before you walk in the door.)

The fact that so many churches are more a health club than an AA meeting is massively dishonoring to the Head of the Church – a Savior who hung out with tax collectors, lepers, prostitutes, and other outcasts.

There is more of this among us than we want to admit. Few voice their judgments – at least to those who are broken – and many go out of their way to be kind and helpful to those who stumble in. Still, there are subtle cues sent out that "this is a place for winners."

God have mercy on us.

May we each learn from Jesus and AA about how to show up broken, and how to embrace those who stumble in as well.

Do you welcome the broken and hurting to church?

Consider: 2 Corinthians 4:7-12; Psalm 22

Prayer for the Week – Mother Teresa

> *Dear Jesus, help me to spread thy fragrance everywhere I go. Flood my soul with Thy spirit and love. Penetrate and possess my whole being so utterly that all my life may only be a radiance of Thine. Shine through me and be so in me that every soul I come in contact with may feel Thy presence in my soul. Let them look up and see no longer me but only Jesus. Stay with me and then I shall begin to shine as you shine, so to shine as to be a light to others.*

---

[1] In James 3 we are told that teachers are held to a higher standard. It is quite likely that certain of these sins would disqualify me to serve as pastor. My point is, I do hope I would not hide from my sin, but return to church, repent and be embraced to move forward.

THE BROKEN CLUB

*The world breaks every one and afterward
many are strong at the broken places.*
— ERNEST HEMINGWAY —

*Go out quickly into the streets and alleys of the town
and bring in the poor, the crippled, the blind and the lame. …
Go out to the roads and country lanes and compel them
to come in, so that my house will be full.*
— JESUS, THE GOSPEL OF LUKE —

———————————————————————

After a worship service ends, I usually stand in the back
of the sanctuary and greet people as they file out. One
Sunday shortly after returning from my stroke, I realized
that something odd was happening. I was being particularly
warmly greeted by people who had seldom said anything
to me in the past. Finally one young woman helped me
understand what was going on. A single mom who had had
an unusually rough few years leaned close and whispered
into my ear, "Welcome to The Broken Club."

The Broken Club?

The Broken Club?

I had no idea that such a group existed, but as soon as she welcomed me into it I saw the group's members all around me. It was so startling that I almost uttered Haley Joel Osment's iconic line, "I see dead people." Only instead, I would have said, "I see *broken people*."

If you're not yet a member, here's the deal. There is an empathy-network out there made up of the most damaged – and the most grace-filled – people in the room. It's all around you, but it's only visible under certain conditions.

- **First, you have to *be* profoundly broken.**
  Everyone qualifies for membership in *The Broken Club* because of sin.[1] It's the least exclusive club in history. But realizing your spiritual need is seldom enough. You generally have to be broken in other ways as well – emotionally, financially, physically, relationally, etc. – in order to begin to grasp the depth of your spiritual condition.

- **Second, you have to *admit* that you are broken.**
  This starts by admitting as much to yourself, but it extends to admitting as much to others. In fact, to earn your membership card you have to be done acting like you've got things together. You have to have thrown your game face away.[2] This seldom happens. We really like to be viewed as winners and put the mask back on as soon as we are able.

I'm glad I finally learned about *The Broken Club*. It's one of the most honest, loving and grace-filled groups around. Much of our life is focused on performance. The Broken Club is not. Like the Kingdom of God, it's much more like a party.

As I hope I've made clear, everyone is invited, even those who are broken.

Especially those who are broken.[3]

Your invitation awaits.

What is the value in being part of the "Broken Club"?

Consider: Romans 3:23; Romans 6:23

Prayer for the Week – Mother Teresa

> *Dear Jesus, help me to spread thy fragrance everywhere I go. Flood my soul with Thy spirit and love. Penetrate and possess my whole being so utterly that all my life may only be a radiance of Thine. Shine through me and be so in me that every soul I come in contact with may feel Thy presence in my soul. Let them look up and see no longer me but only Jesus. Stay with me and then I shall begin to shine as you shine, so to shine as to be a light to others.*

---

[1] Spiritually speaking we are all broken. As Paul wrote in his letter to the Church in Rome, "We all have sinned and fall short of the glory of God." (Romans 3:23) We are all sinners, thus we are all broken.

[2] This doesn't mean we bleed all over everyone we see, but it does mean that we are transparent with some. And like Hemingway suggests, the choice is not between being broken or not, but whether we become "strong at the broken places". (Ernest Hemingway, *A Farewell to Arms* [1929; Simon and Schuster, 1997], p. 226.)

[3] Recall Jesus' important teaching in Luke 14:15-24: When one of those at the table with him heard this, he said to Jesus, "Blessed is the one who will eat at the feast in the kingdom of God." Jesus replied: "A certain man was preparing a great banquet and invited many guests. At the time of the banquet he sent his servant to tell those who had been invited, 'Come, for everything is now ready.' "But they all alike began to make excuses. The first said, 'I have just bought a field, and I must go and see it. Please excuse me.' "Another said, 'I have just bought five yoke of oxen, and I'm on my way to try them out. Please excuse me.' "Still another said, 'I just got married, so I can't come.' "The servant came back and reported this to his master. Then the owner of the house became angry and ordered his servant, 'Go out quickly into the streets and alleys of the town and bring in the poor, the crippled, the blind and the lame.' "'Sir,' the servant said, 'what you ordered has been done, but there is still room.' "Then the master told his servant, 'Go out to the roads and country lanes and compel them to come in, so that my house will be full. I tell you, not one of those who were invited will get a taste of my banquet.'" (Luke 14:15-24)

BURDEN

*The truly strong person is not the one
who never needs help,
but the one who can ask for it when he does.*

— ANONYMOUS —

Having borne a significant amount of the financial burden
for his parents during their declining years, my dad was
determined never to become a drain on his children. And
he told us as much in a variety of ways. In fact, during the
last twenty years of his life he repeatedly assured us that all
of the expenses he (or my Mom) might ever incur were fully
funded and that he had set aside enough money to care for
my mom for as long as she might live.

My reaction – as well as that of my siblings – was to roll our
eyes. None of us had to be told that he had their expenses
accounted for. This was a man who had me saving for
college before I knew what college was. Furthermore, the
conversations he initiated after 1970 were either about
Michigan State football or our need to put more money into
a 401K plan.

We rolled our eyes mostly because we knew we didn't need to worry. But we also rolled them because we wanted to help. In fact, I feel a little cheated that I was never able to do so.

I understand why he did what he did. It was an act of love from someone who grew up very poor. And I appreciate it. Furthermore, the last six months have allowed me to feel what it's like to take without giving. It's no fun to be dependent on others. I understand why he didn't want to go out that way.

But can you ever be a burden to someone who loves you? Is that really the right word?

Anglican priest Giles Fraser captures my thoughts perfectly when he writes:

> Many people express desire not to be a burden on their family when they are dying. I do want to be a burden on my loved ones just as I want them to be a burden on me – it's called looking after each other … My existence is fundamentally bound up with yours…Of course, I will hold your hand in the long hours of the night. Shut up about being a burden. I love you. This is what it means to love you. Surely, there is something extraordinarily beautiful about all of this.[1]

Have you helped someone "carry their burden" recently?

Consider: Galatians 6:1-2; John 13:34-35

Prayer for the Week – Mother Teresa

> *Dear Jesus, help me to spread thy fragrance everywhere I go. Flood my soul with Thy spirit and love. Penetrate and possess my whole being so utterly that all my life may only be a radiance of Thine. Shine through me and be so in me that every soul I come in contact with may feel Thy presence in my soul. Let them look up and see no longer me but only Jesus. Stay with me and then I shall begin to shine as you shine, so to shine as to be a light to others.*

---

[1] *Christian Century*, June 3 2013

CARPE DIEM

Be very careful, then, how you live –
not as unwise but as wise, making the most of every
opportunity, because the days are evil.

— THE APOSTLE PAUL —

A crisis is a terrible thing to waste.

— PAUL ROMER —

Choose to view life through God's eyes. This will not be easy
because it doesn't come naturally to us.
We cannot do this on our own. We have to allow God
to elevate our vantage point. Start by reading His Word,
the Bible...Pray and ask God to transform your thinking.
Let Him do what you cannot.
Ask Him to give you an eternal, divine perspective.

— CHARLES R. SWINDOLL —

Jim Collins, the management guru, has determined that
one of the characteristics of great organizations is that they
leverage luck. As someone who believes in the providence
of God, I don't give a lot of credence to luck. But I think that
Collins is on to something.

The Greek's made a distinction between two kinds of time: *chronos* and *kairos*. *Chronos*, which gives us *chronology*, is used to describe normal time – i.e., seconds, minutes and hours. *Kairos* refers to special, unique moments – the ones that make all the difference.

I read somewhere that a college football game is made up of about one hundred plays, but the outcome hinges on three or four. Those three or four are *kairos* moments.

We are fools to let *kairos* moments get away.

A crisis is always a *kairos* moment. We can grow more in a crisis than in a month of Sundays.

Seize the crisis.

What do you think greatness looks like for your life?

Consider: Ecclesiastes 5:1-4; Proverbs 6:6-11

Prayer for the Week – Thomas Merton

> *Dear God, I have no idea where I am going. I do not see the road ahead of me. I cannot know for certain where it will end. Nor do I really know myself, and the fact that I think I am following your will does not mean that I am actually doing so. But I believe that my desire to please you does in fact please you. I hope that I have that desire in everything that I do. I hope that I will never do anything apart from that desire. And I know that if I do this you will lead me by the right road though I may know nothing about it. Therefore, I will trust you always though I may seem to be lost in the shadow of death. I will not fear, for you are always with me, and you will never leave me to face my troubles alone.*

CHILDREN

*Before I married, I had three theories about raising children
and no children. Now, I have three children and no theories.*

— JOHN WILMOT —

*So Joshua called together the twelve men he had appointed
from the Israelites, one from each tribe, and said to them,
"Go over before the ark of the LORD your God into the
middle of the Jordan. Each of you is to take up a stone on
his shoulder, according to the number of the tribes of the
Israelites, to serve as a sign among you. In the future, when
your children ask you, 'What do these stones mean?'
tell them that the flow of the Jordan was cut off before the
ark of the covenant of the LORD. When it crossed the Jordan,
the waters of the Jordan were cut off. These stones are to be a
memorial to the people of Israel forever."*

— JOSHUA 4:21 —

The other night we were having dinner with friends who are
also moving through a season of hardship. During the meal
she (the wife and mother) said something quite memorable,
"At each turn of the crisis we've been reminding each other,
'remember, the children are watching.'"

The question is not, "Will we get knocked down?" We will. The question is, "How will we respond when we do?" Our response may be more important than the trial itself, because while we cannot always control the trial, we can control our response.

What are your children learning from you?

What lessons would you want to impart to your children?

Consider: Joshua 4:4-7; Deuteronomy 6:4-9

Prayer for the Week – Thomas Merton

> *Dear God, I have no idea where I am going. I do not see the road ahead of me. I cannot know for certain where it will end. Nor do I really know myself, and the fact that I think I am following your will does not mean that I am actually doing so. But I believe that my desire to please you does in fact please you. I hope that I have that desire in everything that I do. I hope that I will never do anything apart from that desire. And I know that if I do this you will lead me by the right road though I may know nothing about it. Therefore, I will trust you always though I may seem to be lost in the shadow of death. I will not fear, for you are always with me, and you will never leave me to face my troubles alone.*

CHOICES

You have brains in your head. You have feet in your shoes.
You can steer yourself in any direction you choose.
You're on your own, and you know what you know.
And you are the guy who'll decide where to go.

— DR. SEUSS —

Now fear the LORD and serve him with all faithfulness.
Throw away the gods your ancestors worshiped beyond the
Euphrates River and in Egypt, and serve the LORD.
But if serving the LORD seems undesirable to you,
then choose for yourselves this day whom you will serve,
whether the gods your ancestors served beyond the
Euphrates, or the gods of the Amorites, in whose land you are
living. But as for me and my household,
we will serve the LORD.

— JOSHUA 24:14-15 —

Not long before the stroke, I stopped by the grocery store on the way home from the office to pick up a few things. On the list was 'Kraft, Italian, Light' salad dressing. (You might see where this is headed).

I could find 'Kraft, Italian, regular' dressing. I could find

'Kraft, Italian, zesty' dressing. I could find 'Kraft, Italian, No Fat,' as well as 'Kraft French Light' and 'Hidden Valley, Italian, light.' But I could not find 'Kraft, Italian Light,' dressing. There must have been three hundred different options and I could find everything except what I was looking for.

We live in a world of choices. If you think I'm wrong, pick any category of food – e.g., cereal, soft drink, cheese, ice cream, potato chips, etc., and then head to the grocery store to do your own research. You want a Diet Coke? Will a Diet Pepsi do? If not, what kind of Diet Coke did you want: regular, cherry, lime or caffeine free; bottle or can; six oz., twelve oz. or liter?

We live in a world of choices, but most of the choices in front of us add little to our life other than confusion and stress.

That said, some choices do matter. For instance, we get to choose what defines us. I'm not suggesting that we have to pick between the roles we play. I am at once a husband, father, brother, son, friend, pastor, neighbor, Christ-follower, runner, reader and more.

I am approaching the matter of choices from a different vantage point. Let me explain: for a while it felt like my medical problems defined me. I was a stroke victim, period, full stop. That is what mattered most. In fact, it felt like when people looked at me that is what they saw. It took a very deliberate decision on my part to decide that I was not my medical challenges. My stroke would not be the last word or the most important thing that could be said about me. What mattered most about me was that I was – I am! – a child of God. I was made in his image and redeemed by the death of his Son. I was chosen by him before the foundations of the world.[1]

How are you defining yourself? As a cancer patient? An alcoholic? A divorcee? Do you think of yourself as "the man who was fired?" or "the woman who was cheated on?" Something else? What do you see when you look in the mirror?

The tragedies we endure briefly block out all of the sun, but they will recede if we let them. For a while they are our story, but over time they become just a part of our story. We get to choose what defines us.

Choose wisely.

What descriptions or words most define who you are?

Consider: Joshua 24:14-18; John 3:1-21

Prayer for the Week – Thomas Merton

> *Dear God, I have no idea where I am going. I do not see the road ahead of me. I cannot know for certain where it will end. Nor do I really know myself, and the fact that I think I am following your will does not mean that I am actually doing so. But I believe that my desire to please you does in fact please you. I hope that I have that desire in everything that I do. I hope that I will never do anything apart from that desire. And I know that if I do this you will lead me by the right road though I may know nothing about it. Therefore, I will trust you always though I may seem to be lost in the shadow of death. I will not fear, for you are always with me, and you will never leave me to face my troubles alone.*

---

[1] Ephesians 1:4

COHERENCE

*The men of Issachar, who understood the times
and knew what Israel should do.*

— I CHRONICLES 12:32 —

Somewhere around week three I realized that something
was missing, but I couldn't identify it. The idea that
anything was being unattended to seemed impossible.
I had four teams of doctors caring for me: neurologists,
neurosurgeons, critical care specialists and rehabilitation
experts. And in addition to aids, barbers, chaplains,
dieticians, insurance advocates, nurses, phlebotomists
and psychologists, I had an army of therapists – e.g.: art
therapists, canine therapists, music therapists, occupational
therapists, speech and physical therapists and probably a
few I am forgetting.[1]

But something was missing. What was it?

And then it hit me. Everyone saw a piece of me, but no one
saw me, and I am more than the sum of my parts. Even with
all of the attention I was receiving, I felt invisible. I was being
overlooked.

Eventually I decided it wasn't the hospital's fault. All of my caregivers were being kind and thoughtful. They were doing their job as they understood it, and some of the doctors and nurses clearly saw me as something more than "the vestibular dissection in room 806."

They were not the problem. The problem was (is) us. We have divided everything into tiny parts. It's all specialists, sub-specialists and sub-sub-specialists with hardly any overlap. No one sees the whole. A is distinct from B; faith doesn't overlap with science; Sunday doesn't affect Monday, and there are times when Monday morning doesn't appear to have much to do with Monday night.

Few See the Whole

In an effort to understand how the world works we've divided it into thousands of pieces. This has certain advantages – such as my ability to get the specific help I need from a neuro-optometrist and an otolaryngologist. The problem is, few now see the big picture and even fewer seem to try.

The Balkanization[2] of life is particularly easy to see when we look at higher education. Back when Harvard was founded, the college experience was not just rigorously Christian; it was purposefully integrated as well.[3] Everything tied together. In fact, the final course a student took – which was taught by the president of the school – was specifically designed to help him or her assimilate everything they had learned into a coherent philosophy of life. The goal of the university was specific: they wanted to turn students into ideal citizens, astute disciples of Christ and virtuous people.[4]

If you've attended college in the last fifty years, you know this is no longer the case. And it's not just because universities no longer embrace a Christian worldview, it's that there is no coherent worldview left to impart.[5]

And few seem to mind.

Let me pause again to note several things:

- There are some advantages to the way we are doing things. (I am the grateful recipient of wonderful care from brilliant doctors who have spent decades learning everything they can about various aspects of the brain.)

- I believe higher education is still one of the best ways to turn an otherwise under-informed (and unemployable) 18 year old into a working adult.

- There were problems with the "good old days."[6]

However, the path we have wandered down has some real downsides. We now not only lack an agreed upon understanding of life, we lack a unified vision of life. I am not sure how to "fix" this; nor am I optimistic that higher education could even if it wanted to.[7] I'm just making an observation. Sometimes it's easy to see the cracks in Modernity. Being overlooked by thirty different specialists is one of them.

Is there a central purpose that gives your life coherence?

Consider: 1 Chronicles 12:32; Colossians 1:15-20

Prayer for the Week – Thomas Merton

> *Dear God, I have no idea where I am going. I do not see the road ahead of me. I cannot know for certain where it will end. Nor do I really know myself, and the fact that I think I am following your will does not mean that I am actually doing so. But I believe that my desire to please you does in fact please you. I hope that I have that desire in everything that I do. I hope that I will never do anything apart from that desire. And I know that if I do this you will lead me by the right road though I may know nothing about it. Therefore, I will trust you always though I may seem to be lost in the shadow of death. I will not fear, for you are always with me, and you will never leave me to face my troubles alone.*

---

[1] The stroke / brain injury hospital where I spent three weeks recovering has a national reputation for excellence, so I in no way want to disparage the care I received. It was quite remarkable. In fact, I felt guilty ending up at such a facility. It seemed to me that even in the midst of suffering I had quickly returned to a position of privilege.

[2] Balkanization, is a term used to describe the process of fragmentation or division into smaller units that are often hostile or non-cooperative with one another.

[3] John Harvard's charge was explicit: "Let every student be plainly instructed and earnestly pressed to consider well the main ends of his life and studies: to know God and Jesus Christ, which is eternal life; and to lay Christ in the bottom as the only foundation of knowledge and learning, and to see the Lord as the giver of all wisdom. Let everyone seriously set himself by prayer in secret to see Christ as Lord and Master." Other schools – e.g., William & Mary, Yale, Princeton, Rutgers, Brown and more – had similar ideals. Indeed, education remained an almost exclusively Christian enterprise up until Abraham Lincoln signed the Morrill Act in 1862, which provided land for modern universities. But even after that the church's role in education was profound. In 1840, 67 percent of state universities had ministers serving as presidents. And in 1885, a University of Illinois student was expelled from the school for willfully missing compulsory chapel. Things were quite different. Developing virtuous people – as defined by The Bible – was the goal. To that end the president was almost always a prominent pastor, chapel was required and the education students received was both Christian and coherent.

[4] The capstone of the college experience in those days (early 19th century) was a year-long course, often taught by the college president in 'moral philosophy' or 'mental science.' It was a course with vast horizons, much as Witherspoon (1723-1794), was the President of Princeton. Mark Noll suggests that Witherspoon did more than any other person to bring Christian higher education into line with the new cultural convictions of American society at that time. [Mark Noll, "Christian Colleges, Christian Worldviews, and An Invitation to Research, *An Introduction to William Ringenberg's The Christian College*, page 12]. had set it out, including everything having to do with human beings and their social relations (the subjects to be studied under this rubric would later become the separate disciplines of psychology, philosophy, religion, political science, sociology, anthropology, economics, and jurisprudence). The course almost always included an investigation of epistemology in general and the epistemological

foundations of Christianity in particular. The purpose of the course was to provide final Christian integration for the college career and final exhortations concerning the kind of citizenship good Christians should practice. (Mark Noll, page 18 of The Christian College by Ringenberg.)

[5] Forget trying to establish common ground between the humanities and the hard sciences, few within the humanities agree on much.

[6] Most people who pine for the good old days have a short memory. They are also almost certainly a white male. While I do feel that some aspects of current culture reflect a moral decay, some things are better – e.g., it was certainly a good idea to end segregation and Jim Crow Laws.

[7] I am not optimistic that higher education could resume their mission of forming upstanding, morally formed and rigorously integrated people for several reasons. One of them is this: they no longer share an understanding of the world or agree on what constitutes a good person. Universities have rules against cheating on exams (or in sports!), and residence halls have policies against certain illegal activities, but for the most part the university does not consider the formation of a particular kind of character to be their responsibility. If for no other reason than this: at most schools there is no agreement about these matters among the faculty. If a trustee was to stand up at a faculty meeting and assign the faculty the responsibility of cultivating virtuous character in students, the meeting would devolve into an endless debate over what kind of behavior was virtuous. *Who defines character? What morals are we after?* And second – as I have already argued – it's not just that most degrees are increasingly technical, it's that they are so specialized that few ever go to 30,000 feet to try to figure out how the pieces go together. As the joke goes, the longer you go to school the more you learn about less and less until pretty soon you know everything about nothing.

DEATH

Death is no more than passing from one room into another.
But there's a difference for me, you know. Because in that
other room I shall be able to see.

— HELEN KELLER —

To live is Christ and to die is gain.

— THE APOSTLE PAUL —

I wrote the following on June 22, the day after my father died.

> When I woke up this morning I saw that I had a phone message from my brother. He had called at 12:56 AM. I didn't have to wonder why. He had been sitting vigil with my dad. And phones that ring in the middle of the night seldom bring good news.

> I waited a couple hours before calling back, reasoning that if he'd been making calls at 1 AM, he probably wasn't up early. When I reached him he confirmed what I already knew: sometime shortly after midnight my father had "slipped away." The hospice staff said that when they checked on him around midnight he was resting comfortably. When they checked on him

ten minutes later he was gone. They told my mom they were not surprised. They had heard that one more child was due to show up. Their guess was that my dad would hold out until the last of the five kids had been in to say good-bye. Steve, my youngest brother, had arrived on Saturday.

How do we respond to the death of a loved one who knows Christ – and is thus promised eternal life? Some say we rejoice. I protest. That's too simple of an answer. It's not complete.

Death is ugly. It reduced my dad to a shell of who he'd been. The man lying in the hospital bed was not the giant I knew as a child; not the man who hit more homeruns for the company softball team (of which I was the five year old bat boy) than anyone else; not the guy who got up early, worked hard and helped put five kids through college and grad school. Cancer and chemo diminished him. Death destroys. My mom told me that he fought hard to maintain his dignity throughout his fight with cancer. "When he lost that I think he just gave up."

Death is ugly. For those in Christ it has lost its sting, but it is still a sign of the curse. It has been defeated but not yet destroyed. We await that (1 Cor. 15:26f).

It's too simple to say that our response to the death of a Christ-follower is "to rejoice." There is that side of it, and not simply because it brings an end to their suffering, but also because it allows us to leave the world of the dying and enter the land of the living. It allows us to fully enter into the presence of God.

How do we respond to the death of a loved one? I turn to Acts 8:2 for direction. It's an easy passage to overlook but it has much to offer. It comes immediately after the stoning of Stephen. As you may know, shortly after Pentecost the early church grew rapidly and enjoyed great favor with just about everyone….but then the persecution began. There was a 300 year, Empire-wide effort to wipe out Christianity. The first victim (martyr) was Stephen. He was stoned.

His death came after he had given an impassioned speech to an agitated mob. For a while it looked as if he had won most of them over. He might have made it out alive had he stopped with the history lesson. But he kept speaking, directing his comments to them. Let me quote from Acts 7:51 and following, which I am taking from Eugene Peterson's paraphrase, *The Message*. This is the end of Stephen's speech:

> "And you continue, so bullheaded! Calluses on your hearts, flaps on your ears! Deliberately ignoring the Holy Spirit, you're just like your ancestors. Was there ever a prophet who didn't

get the same treatment? Your ancestors killed anyone who dared talk about the coming of the Just One. And you've kept up the family tradition—traitors and murderers, all of you. You had God's Law handed to you by angels—gift-wrapped!—and you squandered it!"

At that point they went wild, a rioting mob of catcalls and whistles and invective. But Stephen, full of the Holy Spirit, hardly noticed—he only had eyes for God, whom he saw in all his glory with Jesus standing at his side. He said, "Oh! I see heaven wide open and the Son of Man standing at God's side!"

Yelling and hissing, the mob drowned him out. Now in full stampede, they dragged him out of town and pelted him with rocks.

Stephen died under a shower of rocks. It was quite a way to go out: he offered powerful testimony to the work of Christ; he stood fearless in the face of an angry crowd; he saw Jesus (who was normally seated at the right hand of the Father) stand to welcome him into heaven; and then he died.

How did his friends respond to his death? Acts 8:2 gives us the answer. There we read:

> Godly men buried Stephen and mourned deeply for him.

The translation I first memorized said, "Righteous men buried Stephen and wept."

Did they cry for Stephen? Hardly. The King of the Universe had stood to welcome him into Heaven. They were believers. They knew it was all good for Stephen! They wept for themselves. His gain was their loss.

My dad was not Stephen, and he would be the first to say so. But he was justified by the death of the King of the Universe, and so he has been welcomed into Heaven. There is no need to cry for him. But his gain is our loss. I'm glad his suffering is over, and thankful that he lived until I was in my 50s. Few have that privilege.

But it's OK to weep.

What scares you most about death?

Consider: John 11:32-37; Hebrews 9:27-28

Prayer for the Week – Thomas Merton

> *Dear God, I have no idea where I am going. I do not see the road ahead of me. I cannot know for certain where it will end. Nor do I really know myself, and the fact that I think I am following your will does not mean that I am actually doing so. But I believe that my desire to please you does in fact please you. I hope that I have that desire in everything that I do. I hope that I will never do anything apart from that desire. And I know that if I do this you will lead me by the right road though I may know nothing about it. Therefore, I will trust you always though I may seem to be lost in the shadow of death. I will not fear, for you are always with me, and you will never leave me to face my troubles alone.*

DEATH II

Brothers and sisters, we do not want you to be uninformed about those who sleep in death, so that you do not grieve like the rest of mankind, who have no hope. For we believe that Jesus died and rose again, and so we believe that God will bring with Jesus those who have fallen asleep in him.

— THE APOSTLE PAUL —

The following was shared with me by a grieving widower. His young wife had recently died after an extended battle with cancer. The letter was written by a mutual friend – a man who had recently lost a young son himself. He wrote:

Dear Friend:

We were saddened this morning to hear of our dear ABC's home going and yet we cannot question it. We can only leave our questions to God whose comprehension is beyond our domain.

We instead embrace the promise of a greater reunion in the future as well as the resurrection home and the beauty of heaven though beyond our limited knowledge.

I know that ABC touched many lives, finished her

service and has gone to be with her God. Our tears are but for ourselves for she is home and we are the ones who for a little longer remain in a foreign land.

Our prayer is that through it all you will experience a full portion of God's grace, comfort and peace that defies human understanding. May our Lord minister his peace, patience and security to your soul.

Your brother in Christ and his family,

Contemporary American culture has many upsides, but it does a poor job of teaching us how to think about death.

As the writer of the note observes, eternity changes everything. We grieve for a time, but a great reunion awaits those who are in Christ.

Where do you find courage facing death?

Consider: 1 Thessalonians 4:13-14; Psalm 23

Prayer for the Week – Thomas Merton

> *Dear God, I have no idea where I am going. I do not see the road ahead of me. I cannot know for certain where it will end. Nor do I really know myself, and the fact that I think I am following your will does not mean that I am actually doing so. But I believe that my desire to please you does in fact please you. I hope that I have that desire in everything that I do. I hope that I will never do anything apart from that desire. And I know that if I do this you will lead me by the right road though I may know nothing about it. Therefore, I will trust you always though I may seem to be lost in the shadow of death. I will not fear, for you are always with me, and you will never leave me to face my troubles alone.*

ELDERS

The older I grow, the more I distrust the familiar doctrine that age brings wisdom.

— H.L. MENCKEN —

The wise man does not grow old, but ripens.

— VICTOR HUGO —

The other day I overheard a man lamenting his belief that though there are more elderly people alive today than in the past, there are fewer elders. That is, though we have a growing number of people moving through their 70s and 80s, we have fewer men and women of great stature – i.e., those who are wise, kind and selfless. The man wondered, "Where are the people who have gotten over themselves, who have no agenda other than to help others, who say little but make every word count? Where are the selfless sages?"

For some time I've repeated a phrase I picked up years ago: *not all who grow old grow wise.*

We need more who do. For the last twenty years we have rewarded those who can manipulate data and access information – people who are typically quite young. In the last decade we have increasingly deferred to those who talk loudly (and incessantly) on the radio. We are now drowning in information and blaring voices. What is lacking is wisdom.

We have many elderly but few elders.

Who is in your life to offer you counsel or advice?

Consider: Leviticus 19:32; 1 Timothy 3:1-7

Prayer for the Week – John Wesley

> *O that we could begin this day in devout meditations, in joy unspeakable, and in blessing and praising Thee, who has given us such good hope and everlasting consolation. Lift up our minds above all these little things below, which are apt to distract our thoughts; and keep them above till our hearts are fully bent to seek Thee every day, in the way wherein Jesus hath gone before us.*

ENCOURAGEMENT

Instruction does much, but encouragement everything.
— JOHANN WOLFGANG VON GOETHE —

Be kind, for every person you meet is fighting a great battle.
— IAN MACLAREN —

I have two files labeled encouragement, one contains articles about the topic and the other has cards, emails and letters sent to encourage me. I started the second one about ten years ago, thinking that one day I'd be discouraged and need a pick-me up. At the time I thought reading old notes might be helpful.

So far it hasn't happened. I've been discouraged plenty of times, but reading old notes has yet to seem like a helpful idea. I'm not wired that way. I care a good deal about the opinions of a few others – especially Sheri, and (before his death) my Dad. But I tend to be pretty internally governed. If I think I've messed up and you think I've done well, your words of affirmation are unlikely to make me feel any better. Likewise, if you think I'm an idiot (and write and tell me so), but I think I'm doing pretty well, I'll listen but I'm unlikely to change my course.

I'm not saying that my way is right, I'm just setting the context. What I want you to hear is this: I am not typically moved by casual words of encouragement.

But I sure was during my recovery!

To my great surprise, I invested an embarrassing amount of meaning in the passing comments made by just about anyone.

> "Good morning Mr. Woodruff. You're looking good today. I think you are sitting up much straighter than last week."

> "Mr. Woodruff, I saw you walking laps with your therapist yesterday. Wow. You're going to be running these halls soon."

Even as I write these I recognize that they were mostly throw-away lines. There were times when my therapists went over my progress with data and offered concrete affirmation, but the comments I am referencing here were casual, almost flippant, perhaps even patronizing. But I soaked them up. They gave me hope at a time when I desperately needed it.

I suspect my pride kept me from revealing just how much these comments meant to me at the time, but I am not sure I could have been happier if you told me I'd just won a Nobel Prize. *I'm sitting up straighter today! How about me! I'm walking faster than before! I'll bet I can stand on my own by this weekend.*

Why am I revealing this rather embarrassing information? *(Is Woodruff really that shallow?)* I am doing so to make two points:

- When people get knocked down, it doesn't take much to encourage them. All they need is a little hope.
- Imparting hope is often easy to do and costs very little.

Do you think I am wrong? Here's a second example. After news of my stroke spread through the ranks of my former fraternity brothers, a number of them wrote me notes of affirmation and encouragement. One went so far as to print them all out and send them to me in a font large enough that even I could read them.

For the most part, reading their reflections felt like eavesdropping on my own funeral,[1] but what stands out most is the note from a man who graduated a couple years ahead of me. I do not remember the call he describes, but apparently he called the fraternity house one night when he was quite discouraged. He had graduated a year earlier and was now in a particularly challenging section of military training. I was the one who answered the phone, and we ended up talking for twenty minutes, during which time I filled him in on what was happening at the "Tool Shed" –

our nickname for the fraternity house. He claims the phone call made a big difference in his outlook and helped him survive the next phase of his training, which involved "jumping out of a perfectly good airplane over and over for no good reason at all!"

When I read his kind words I was thrilled to learn that our brief phone call had made a difference to him. But I was also shaken by it, for I know how easily I might have cut him off because I was too busy – i.e., too important – to "waste time talking on the phone." Of course I would never have done so if I had any idea how important the phone call would turn out to be. But we seldom are privileged with that information in advance.

When life is working, the casual affirmations of others may not make much of a difference to us. But when we are hurting, those words can be like a glass of cold water to someone dying of thirst.

Who can you affirm today?

Who will you encourage today with your words or actions?

Consider: Hebrews 3:12-14; Titus 2:6-8

Prayer for the Week – John Wesley

> *O that we could begin this day in devout meditations, in joy unspeakable, and in blessing and praising Thee, who has given us such good hope and everlasting consolation. Lift up our minds above all these little things below, which are apt to distract our thoughts; and keep them above till our hearts are fully bent to seek Thee every day, in the way wherein Jesus hath gone before us.*

---

[1] I suspect that some of my fraternity brothers will want to retract the kind things they said about me now that I have recovered.

FATHERS AND SONS

As soon as Jesus was baptized, he went up out of the water.
At that moment heaven was opened, and he saw the Spirit
of God descending like a dove and alighting on him.
And a voice from heaven said, "This is my Son,
whom I love; with him I am well pleased."

— MATTHEW 3:16-17 —

Not quite a year before my father died, he and my Mom called to let me know that he'd just been diagnosed with an aggressive form of leukemia. Although he would survive for nearly a year, at the time of the call, the doctor's best guess was that he had four to six weeks to live.

I wrote about some of this in Book One, *Are You Ready to be Broken?* so I will not repeat it here, other than to say this: I am profoundly blessed by the chance to have a great ending conversation with my Dad.

Shortly after arriving at my parents I noticed that my Dad had slipped away from the rest of the family and was sitting alone on the back deck, so I went out to join him. My Dad was never one to put off anything unpleasant. (He'd been known to mow the grass in the rain simply because "It needs to be done and there's no time like the present to do what needs to be done.") So I was caught only slightly off guard when he immediately brought up something I'd said in a Father's Day sermon a few months earlier. In a message on the power of a father's words, I'd told a story about a phone message he had left on our home answering machine a few years earlier.

I do not remember the reason he called, or the rest of the message he left, but he ended by saying, "That's all for now. I love you and I'm proud of you. We'll talk later."

The first time I heard the message I was stunned. For starters, my Dad didn't call me. In fact, since I left for college in 1978, I doubt he'd called me more than ten times. That was not the way things worked. I called my parents every week, and if my Dad happened to answer the phone we chatted for about fifteen seconds while he found my Mom. He didn't really do the phone.

Secondly, I'm quite sure he'd never ended a conversation with me by saying, "I love you and I'm proud of you." I was so shocked by his words that I'd played them over and over. I then saved them for the better part of a year, playing them every other week or so just to hear him say, "I love you and I'm proud of you."

In the sermon I recounted this story and reported on the hoops I had jumped through to keep the phone company from erasing the message. But then one day Sheri had called and said, "The message you've been saving is about to be deleted. The 100 day extension is up. What do you want to do? I don't know what this message is about. But I know you've been saving it."

I told her that she could let it lapse and then – as best I could through my tears – I told her about the call. I ended by saying, "I am mystified by the power those words have over me."

In the sermon I'd gone on to note that I grew up thinking that nothing I ever did was good enough for him. I felt that he pushed way too hard and demanded way too much. I also reported how I'd had to work pretty hard in my thirties to work through my mixed emotions about him.

My Dad and I had never really had a conversation about this. It was not the kind of conversation you had with my Dad. I assumed he knew all of this – "how could he not!" – but I'd never brought it up with him. And in fact, I'd gone to some length to make sure he did not hear this particular sermon.[1] But somehow he had. Apparently my Mom had found it on line, listened to it and then told him that he needed to listen to the sermon even though he was not going to like it. He had and was now bringing it up.

As soon as he brought up the sermon I felt sick. My next thought was, "This is incredible. I'm 53 years old. He is dying and in one of our last conversations I am going to get in trouble."

But rather than say anything harsh, my Dad started to cry. And then he apologized. He said that he remembered things differently and that he always assumed that I knew he was proud of me. He also said that he pushed as hard as he did because he loved me and he thought it was for my best, but he now wished that he could go back and do it differently. He then reiterated that he did love me and was very proud of me.

I thanked him for his apology and then apologized to him for the ways I had made things worse. I then thanked him for how hard he had worked to support us and for the many good things he had done. By this time I was crying as well. (If the rest of the family saw us, they left us alone. Having not seen either of us cry in years – let alone both of us crying at the same time – they were probably not anxious to step in to what was going on).

My Dad and I spent another fifteen minutes talking before we agreed that everything that needed to be said had been said and that it was all good. As we ended, my Dad told me again that he loved me and was proud of me.

A few hours later I called Sheri and filled her in on the conversation. I remembering stating, "This trip has been a great success. I've heard everything I need to hear. I don't know how things could end on a better note."

I cannot speak firsthand about father-daughter relationships, nor do I have any insights about mother-son or mother-daughter dynamics. But I know this, a father should never underestimate the power his words have to bless or frustrate his boys.

And I close with this observation. One of the very few New Testament records we have of God the Father speaking audibly from heaven is when he says:

> This is my Son, whom I love; with him I am well pleased.

What is the impact your father has had in your life?

Consider: Proverbs 2; John 10:25-32

Prayer for the Week – John Wesley

> *O that we could begin this day in devout meditations, in joy unspeakable, and in blessing and praising Thee, who has given us such good hope and everlasting consolation. Lift up our minds above all these little things below, which are apt to distract our thoughts; and keep them above till our hearts are fully bent to seek Thee every day, in the way wherein Jesus hath gone before us.*

---

[1] A few year earlier I had shared this story in a talk at Men's Fraternity, but I had made sure it was not recorded so there was no chance he could hear it. I had been reluctant to include it in a sermon that I knew would go online, but enough men had told me how helpful it was to them, that I had decided to include the story.

FIFTY

*It's ironic that in our culture everyone's biggest complaint
is about not having enough time; yet nothing terrifies us more
than the thought of eternity.*

— DENNIS MILLER —

*As winter strips the leaves from around us,
so that we may see the distant regions they formerly
concealed, so old age takes away our enjoyments
only to enlarge the prospect of the coming eternity.*

— JEAN PAUL —

My Dad died a few days shy of his 81st birthday. One day near the end, he opened his eyes, looked at me and whispered, "They say that eighty is the new sixty. Don't believe them! They are wrong. Eighty is the same old eighty."

After my last six months, I'm inclined to think that fifty is the new eighty.

But what of it? I write that as if it's a bad thing. Is it? In his letter to the Philippians the Apostle Paul wrote:

> For to me, to live is Christ *and to die is gain*. If I am to go on living in the body, this will mean fruitful labor for me. Yet what shall I choose? I do not know! I am torn

between the two: I desire to depart and be with Christ, which is better by far; but it is more necessary for you that I remain in the body. Convinced of this, I know that I will remain, and I will continue with all of you for your progress and joy in the faith, so that through my being with you again your boasting in Christ Jesus will abound on account of me.

Paul writes as one who understands that this is the land of the dying, and that in Christ we are allowed into the land of the living. This world is broken; Heaven works perfectly. The only reason Paul appears willing to stick around is to extend Christ's kingdom by serving others.

Since the stroke, fifty has seemed a lot closer to eighty than to twenty. But maybe that is a good thing.

What gives your life meaning?

Consider: Philippians 1:21-26; Ecclesiastes 3:9-14

Prayer for the Week – John Wesley

> *O that we could begin this day in devout meditations, in joy unspeakable, and in blessing and praising Thee, who has given us such good hope and everlasting consolation. Lift up our minds above all these little things below, which are apt to distract our thoughts; and keep them above till our hearts are fully bent to seek Thee every day, in the way wherein Jesus hath gone before us.*

FREEDOM

*Nearly all people live in slavery for the reason the Spartans
gave us as the cause of slavery of the Persians:
they are not able to utter the syllable 'no.'*

— NICHOLAS CHAMFORT —

The truth will set you free.

— JESUS, THE GOSPEL OF JOHN —

Americans love their freedom. They celebrate it, champion it
and come very close to deifying it. However, most of us also
misunderstand it. We confuse 'freedom of' with 'freedom
from.' And that is trouble, because they are virtually
opposites.

'Freedom of' refers to the benefits that follow discipline.
Those who tirelessly practice scales on the piano are free to
create beautiful music. Athletes who lift weights, run drills
and watch film are free to perform at the highest levels.

'Freedom from' refers to the opportunity to do nothing – to
sleep in and play video games, to despise discipline and
avoid hard work.

Many today choose to be 'free from' responsibility, but then express frustration (or confusion) when they do not enjoy the freedom to perform great music or win on the field.

Few enjoy rehab – wheelchair aerobics, slow walks down the same halls and balance exercises that are boring and frustrating. But the freedom I want is only available if I embrace the 'freedom of' discipline.

There is a spiritual parallel. In James 1:25 we read that the perfect law [of God] leads to freedom. Indeed it does. A train isn't free when it jumps the tracks. It is free when it does what it was made to do.

The same holds for you and me. We are the most free when we obey God.

Do you tend to see God's wisdom as freeing or confining?

Consider: 1 Peter 2:13-17; 1 Corinthians 10:23-26

Prayer for the Week – John Wesley

> *O that we could begin this day in devout meditations, in joy unspeakable, and in blessing and praising Thee, who has given us such good hope and everlasting consolation. Lift up our minds above all these little things below, which are apt to distract our thoughts; and keep them above till our hearts are fully bent to seek Thee every day, in the way wherein Jesus hath gone before us.*

GIFT

*Healthy children will not fear life if their elders
have integrity enough not to fear death.*

— ERIK ERIKSON —

The fear of death is one of the most common fears of man.
In fact, I think it eclipses just about everything except public
speaking, which I – a public speaker – find comical. Although
I do hate to "die" in front of a group, which happens every
time a joke fails, like right now.

But I'm not trying to make jokes here. I have two points:
death is a big fear, and the way my dad faced his own death
was a gift to his family. Let me explain.

I was present at the meeting where the doctor explained to
my dad how and when he could expect to die. After doing
so, he asked my dad if he had any questions or concerns. My
dad said that he was not scared of death, but then added,
"but I am a bit anxious about the actual dying part."

His doctor assured him that this was understandable and
then promised my Dad that he would do just fine, after all,
everybody dies. No one fails dying. (OK, Jesus sort of failed

dying, but you get the point). He then assured my dad that his death would not be painful. In fact he said, "I promise that you will have a peaceful death," which is, in fact, how he eventually died.

I was not sure how my dad was processing everything the doctor had said to him, but later that day we had a second profound and helpful conversation. It started when he said, "There are no bad endings from here. I do not want anybody to cry for me. I've had a good life. I didn't expect to live this long. Your mom is well off. All five of you kids are doing well. I am in a no-lose situation. If I die I go to heaven. If I live there are people I love and things I still enjoy doing. I do not want anybody crying for me."

No one who knew my dad would be surprised by the very matter-of-fact way he treated his own death, or that he had everything all buttoned up. In the last year of his life my parents had downsized a second time; my dad had bought my mom a new car; he had distributed his few prize possessions – mostly slide rules; and he had left written instructions on everything from the details of his funeral service to when to change the furnace filter.

There is something to be said for all of this. As a pastor I'm occasionally called in to bring order when none of these things have been attended to. I've also been asked to broker peace when the will has contained big surprises, pitting children against children, or children against step-mothers. I appreciate the fact that my dad was thoughtful enough to attend to all of this.

But what I appreciated most was the way he went out. His level of calm did not – could not – take away all of the pain or tears, but it was sure a lot easier for me to watch him go after he had said, "There are no bad endings for me from this point on."

I realize that there are bad endings, and also premature endings. As a dad myself, I just now feel like it would not be irresponsible of me to die, and my youngest son is 20. I cannot imagine the anguish a young mom (or dad) feels when they realize that they will not be there to bandage every skinned knee or kiss away every tear. It's not possible for every person to leave with everything in the kind of order my dad left it.

I'm simply thankful that he did. It was a gift and a lesson.

How are your choices impacting others?

Consider: 2 Timothy 2:1-7; Proverbs 22:6

Prayer for the Week – John Wesley

> *O that we could begin this day in devout meditations, in joy unspeakable, and in blessing and praising Thee, who has given us such good hope and everlasting consolation. Lift up our minds above all these little things below, which are apt to distract our thoughts; and keep them above till our hearts are fully bent to seek Thee every day, in the way wherein Jesus hath gone before us.*

GRATITUDE

*Sing and make music from your heart to the Lord,
always giving thanks to God the Father for everything,
in the name of our Lord Jesus Christ.*

— THE APOSTLE PAUL —

*Gratitude unlocks the fullness of life. It turns what we have
into enough, and more. It turns denial into acceptance, chaos
to order, confusion to clarity. It can turn a meal into a feast,
a house into a home, a stranger into a friend.*

— MELODY BEATTIE —

During the first few months following the stroke, I found it
pretty easy to maintain a good attitude. I felt close to the
Lord; I believed my struggles were proving to be a good
thing for my family; I was making rapid improvement; and
besides, those around me (in the hospital and at both of the
RIC centers) all had bigger challenges ahead of them than
I did. In the Rehabilitation Institute of Chicago (RIC) gym
where I was working out, I was in the best shape of all.

And then one day it turned. Suddenly I was frustrated by
everything. Rather than being thankful that I could walk, I
was angry that I occasionally stumbled. Rather than being

glad I could see well enough to read, I was frustrated that I couldn't see well enough to drive. I was tired of being dizzy, tired of asking for help and tired of being tired.

When I realized how mad I was I sat down to try to figure out why. What had changed? It didn't take long for things to come into focus: I'd switched from an attitude of gratefulness to an attitude of entitlement. Instead of being thankful that God had spared me from the catastrophic deficits that generally accompany a vestibular dissection, I was frustrated that He allowed me to suffer a stroke at all.

That mental shift from gratitude to entitlement was all that had happened, but it explained everything.

In Paul's first letter to the church in Thessalonica he offers the antidote for a bad mood. There he writes:

> Rejoice always, pray continually, give thanks in all circumstances; for this is God's will for you in Christ Jesus.

How do you do that? Simple, you do it. Rather than being frustrated with all of the traffic, be thankful you have a car. It's not a hassle to have to lose weight, but remarkable that we have such an abundance of food. The Thessalonian's passage noted above doesn't tell us that we have to give thanks "for all circumstances," but "in all circumstances." My assignment – and yours! – is to find the good and be thankful for it. It's not that hard and it actually works.

Matthew Henry, a late 17th century British pastor and noted Bible scholar, gives us a great example of how it's done. In a brief journal entry shortly after he was robbed Henry wrote:

> Let me be thankful, first, because he never robbed me before; second, because although he took my purse, he did not take my life; third, because although he took all I possessed, it was not much; and fourth, because it was I who was robbed, not I who robbed.

The counsel Paul offers works. I enjoy the day much more when I am grateful for the things I can do rather than fixated on the things I cannot.

What are five things you can be grateful for today?

Consider: 1 Thessalonians 5:16-18; Psalm 100

Prayer for the Week – Puritan Prayer

> Lord, high and holy, meek and lowly, You have brought me to the valley of vision where I live in the depths but see You in the heights; hemmed in by mountains of sin I behold Your glory. Let me learn by paradox that the way down is the way up, that to be low is to be high, that the broken heart is the healed heart, that the contrite spirit is the rejoicing spirit, that the repenting soul is the victorious soul, that to have nothing is to possess all, that to bear the cross is to wear the crown, that to give is to receive, that the valley is the place of vision. Lord, in the daytime stars can be seen from the deepest wells, and the deeper the wells the brighter Your stars shine; let me find Your light in my darkness, Your life in my death, Your joy in my sorrow, Your grace in my sin, Your riches in my poverty, Your glory in my valley.

GRIEF

But a mermaid has no tears,
and therefore she suffers so much more.
— HANS CHRISTIAN ANDERSEN, *THE LITTLE MERMAID* —

After a major loss we cycle through a series of emotional responses. In her seminal 1969 book, *On Death and Dying*, Elisabeth Kübler-Ross suggested five different ones: denial, anger, bargaining, depression and acceptance. As I noted earlier, in the recent sermon series I preached at Christ Church I followed the six stages Rick Warren spoke about moving through following the suicide of his mentally ill 27 year old son: shock, sorrow, struggle, surrender, sanctification and service.

Both Kübler-Ross and Warren's models suggest a linear clarity that does not exist in reality, but they make some helpful points.

- Immediately following a major set-back we will become emotionally unsettled.

- Those who regain their bearings do so by traversing a number of fairly predictable stages.

- It is possible to return stronger than before – i.e., kinder, wiser, better, more empathetic.

- Many people do not. They get stuck.

Part of what I learned during the last six months is that emotional pain greatly eclipses physical pain. Those who have tasted both would take a broken bone over a broken heart any day. Grief is much more unpleasant, overwhelming and exhausting than a bad back or a sprained ankle. Grief is joy's opposite.[1]

What follows is hardly a definitive grief-guide, but there may be something here to help you prepare for your world to be rocked and your heart broken.

Grief is normal. Expect it and accept it. This world is broken; consequently things will go wrong. Being surprised when bad things happen doesn't help. Many Christ-followers wrongly assume that their decision to say "yes" to God means they are protected from grief. Not true.[2] Quite the opposite, really. Jesus promised us hardships.

Grieving is neither wrong nor unspiritual. Some accept that things will go wrong, but assume that the proper Christian response is to smile and act like everything is OK. I thought this way for years. But the Bible makes it clear that many who love God also grieve.[3] The Old Testament prophets grieved; King David grieved;[4] the Psalms are full of grief, and Jesus – Jesus! – was reduced to tears on at least one occasion. He also said, "blessed are those who mourn."[5]

Grieving is a choice. We have to choose to "let the pain in." Not everyone does. Some people "stuff it" – either consciously (which we call suppression) or unconsciously (which we call repression). This was my *modus operandi* for quite a while. My family didn't do a lot of emotions when I was growing up, so I didn't learn how to process disappointment in a healthy way. For instance, I believed that crying was a sign of weakness, which meant that those emotions needed to be buried.[6] I also thought that the way to process grief was to work harder so that I got what I wanted – i.e., if someone (something) got in my way, I needed to work harder until I got what I wanted. My approach was socially acceptable but unhealthy all the same. It was also ultimately futile. We cannot overcome every challenge.

Grief will find an outlet. Grief is as persistent as ground water. You might patch every crack in the basement, but the water will eventually find a way in. I was fortunate growing up in that my grief was never so overwhelming that it spilled outside my socially acceptable coping methods. I wasn't cutting myself or self-medicating with alcohol. I simply worked harder and ran farther.[7] As defense mechanisms go, these are pretty tame. (Again, this doesn't mean they were effective or healthy. It just means that I didn't have to avoid the police or hide from the school counselor.)

Major loss that isn't processed goes bad. Grief becomes toxic over time. It leads to depression, anger, debilitating addictions or dysfunctional behavior. This is especially the case for kids who do not have as many emotional tools for processing what is going on.[8] One of the very first counseling appointments I ever conducted was with a college freshman whom I'll call Amber (I do not remember her real name). She was brought to see me by her roommate (who I'll call Lauren). Lauren introduced herself and then immediately pointed to Amber and said, "She can't say 'Mom.'"

Turning to Amber I asked, "What does she mean? You can talk, right? And you can say 'Tom' and 'milk' and 'Mike,' so you can say 'Mom,' but you do not?"

"Right," she said. "I can talk but I can't say 'the M word.'"

"So tell me about your mom," I said.

"She's dead," said Amber. "She died when I was eight."

"I'm very sorry to hear that. I'm sure that was really hard. How did she die?"

"I don't know. We've never talked about it. I'm not sure."

"You've never talked about your mom's death?"

"No. We've never talked about my mom at all. My dad doesn't want to. He doesn't allow it."

There was no reason to dig deeper. Clearly, this young woman's grief had been buried, turned toxic and was now finding an odd outlet: she couldn't even talk about "Mom."

Most situations are not as obvious. I chose this one because it makes my point so clearly: grief is not sin, but it can be trouble. Like anger (and other emotions) it can cause problems if it's mishandled. The emotional pain of loss needs to be expressed or it will ferment. Grieving is the healthy way forward. Crying, mourning and leaning into the pain is good.

God has given us tools to deal with our grief. As I have just suggested, we are not without ways forward. God has given us at least three aids to help us process pain and loss.

- **First, he gave us emotions.** God gave us emotions, such as the ability to cry – which is something no other animal can do. Tears are not the goal, but facing the pain is and tears can help us move through it.

- **Second, he gave us friends.**[9] Grief is healed in community.[10]

- **Third, we have the Psalms.** God has not only given us tears to cry and friends to sort things out, He has given us the prayers to pray when we are filled with grief. Though many think the Book of Psalms is filled only with prayers of thanks and praise, close to half of the psalms are cries of lament. The Psalms are a gift to the grieving.

This world is broken by sin and evil. We should expect to suffer and when we suffer we should expect to grieve.

How is grief different for those having a strong Christian faith?

Consider: 2 Corinthians 4:17-18; John 16:20

Prayer for the Week – Puritan Prayer

Lord, high and holy, meek and lowly, You have brought me to the valley of vision where I live in the depths but see You in the heights; hemmed in by mountains of sin I behold Your glory. Let me learn by paradox that the way down is the way up, that to be low is to be high, that the broken heart is the healed heart, that the contrite spirit is the rejoicing spirit, that the repenting soul is the victorious soul, that to have nothing is to possess all, that to bear the cross is to wear the crown, that to give is to receive, that the valley is the place of vision. Lord, in the daytime stars can be seen from the deepest wells, and the deeper the wells the brighter Your stars shine; let me find Your light in my darkness, Your life in my death, Your joy in my sorrow, Your grace in my sin, Your riches in my poverty, Your glory in my valley.

¹ People process grief differently – men and women often react to the same loss in different ways, and different cultures respond differently as well – but in general those who are grieving say things like: *I don't care. I can't sleep. I can't focus. I don't have any energy. I can't believe God cares about me at all. Everything is gray. I'm sad. All I do is cry. I can't even make small decisions. I have a pit in my stomach.*

² In Mark 4:37 – 40 Jesus tells the disciples to get in a boat, and they set sail for the other side. A big storm comes up, and they fear they will die. Meanwhile Jesus is asleep in the front of the boat. It's a famous passage because when Jesus wakes up he rebukes the storm. Rembrandt's rendition of this scene hangs in the office. I like to look at it to be reminded that you can be right next to Jesus – doing exactly what he told you to do – and caught in such an ugly storm that you are sure you're about to die.

³ There is nothing unspiritual about grief. However, those who know Christ should grieve differently. As we learn in I Thes. 4, Christ-followers do not grieve as those who have no hope. Eternity changes everything. Even when everything in this life is unraveling, we can be assured that nothing in heaven has changed and God's promises about eternal life are still true. Furthermore, those who are in Christ have the Holy Spirit, who is also called "the Comforter." So, again, our grief is different. But... grieving is not wrong. Sadness is not weakness or a sign of poor faith.

⁴ David, a man after God's own heart, wrote a number of psalms. Many of them express his frustration with how things were going: In Psalm 118:5 he says that "he cried out with anguish to God;" in Psalm 38:8 he says: "I am feeble and utterly crushed; I groan in anguish of heart;" in Psalm 22 he opens with the cry Jesus will repeat on the cross, "My God, my God, why have you abandoned me?"

⁵ Jesus grieves. Jesus never sinned – He did not do anything wrong or unhealthy – but he grieved. He wept at the funeral for Lazarus (John 11:33); in Isaiah 53 he is described as "a man of sorrows and acquainted with grief;" in Luke 23 he expresses his anguish over Jerusalem; and in the Sermon on the Mount, he said, "Blessed are those who mourn, for they shall be comforted."

[6] I do not remember all of the circumstances. What I do remember is that I was crying and my dad came into the room and told me that he never wanted to hear me cry again. He was quite mad, and he told me that crying was a pathetic sign of weakness. His message was not, "stuff it" as much as it was "grow up," but in order to grow up by that definition I had to stuff it. And so I did, and I didn't cry again for about fifteen to twenty years. Unfortunately, when you turn off negative emotions you turn off positive ones as well.

[7] Runner's World ran fascinating articles on Zola Budd (Steve Friedman, "After the Fall," *Runner's World*, Oct. 2009) and Frank Shorter (John Brant, "Frank's Story" Runner's World, Oct. 2011). As it turned out, both were running because the physical pain of running was the only way they could find relief from the emotional pain they were suffering. (Budd's family life became intolerable after a sister died and Shorter's father was a monster who abused his kids.)

[8] We tend to stay emotionally stuck at the level at which we are unable to process the grief. This is one of the reasons there are so many adult males who are simply old boys. They are not men because they are emotionally stuck and immature.

[9] Some of you are stuck grieving. Others never grieve. One of the reasons we need good friends – wise friends – is to help us see ourselves. Some of you might need to see a therapist for help with this. Please realize: there is no life without change. There is no change without loss. And there is no loss without pain. We need to face the pain. We need to choose to grieve. We have to allow it in.

[10] Galatians 6:2 reads, "Carry each other's burdens, and in this way you will fulfill the law of Christ." In other words, when you're in pain I'm supposed to help carry your pain. When I'm in pain you're supposed to help carry my pain. And this helps everyone because when we share pain it gets lighter. See also: Romans 12:15: When others are happy, be happy with them. If they're sad, share their sorrow: grief is healed in community. Revealing your feeling is the beginning of healing. We share it with each other. That's what we do in small groups.

HAPPINESS

*Faith like Job's cannot be shaken because
it is a result of having been shaken.*
— RABBI ABRAHAM HESCHEL —

Clap along if you feel like happiness is the truth.
— PHARRELL WILLIAMS —

Americans like to be happy. A lot. Indeed in one recent three month period, over one thousand books came out with happy in the title.[1]

There is nothing wrong with this. But we need to understand two things: suffering can be a good thing; there is a difference between happiness and joy.

One, suffering can be a good thing. Some say life would be better if it was more like a DVD – that is, if we could fast forward through the crummy times. I understand the allure of this. No one likes crummy, nor should they be expected to. In contrast to Buddhism, Christianity teaches that suffering is real; in contrast to karma, Christianity teaches that suffering is often unfair. Furthermore, the Christian faith does not suggest that we can work off our moral debt through suffering, nor does it teach that ascetic, voluntary self-afflicted pain makes us more spiritual.[2] As it turns out, there are few upsides and more than a few downsides to suffering. I understand the allure of being able to fast forward through the crummy times.

However, unlike the secularism which prevails so much of Western life today, Christianity suggests that suffering can have meaning – i.e., that those who suffer can be more than victims; they can grow and mature. In fact, a trial can be the chariot that carries them forward. This is the thinking behind the famous opening James pens in his letter:

> Consider it pure joy, my brothers and sisters, whenever you face trials of many kinds, because you know that the testing of your faith produces perseverance. Perseverance must finish its work so that you may be mature and complete, not lacking anything.

Two, there is a distinction between happiness and joy. Though many use *happiness* and *joy* interchangeably, it's helpful to recognize a distinction: happiness is tethered to comfort and pleasure, while joy is linked to spiritual wellbeing. Happiness happens when things are easy and fun; joy occurs as the byproduct of a life rightly lived.[3]

Given this distinction we can imagine someone who is happy but lacks joy (e.g., someone who has every toy available and plays all day, but is deeply unsatisfied with their life) and vice versa (e.g., someone who faces many challenges but who has great friends, a positive attitude and a peaceful heart).

Please understand, I am not trying to disparage happiness. Go to the party! Eat the ice cream cone! Play golf! There is little downside to being happy! But do not build your life around it because that doesn't work. Happiness is too fickle, too shallow and too saccharine to stand up to the rough and tumble of life. A steady diet of happy is like a steady diet of cotton candy. It leaves much to be desired. In contrast to happiness, joy is more substantial. It can weather situations that happiness cannot.[4]

After learning about my stroke a friend wrote to encourage me. A few years ago he nearly died from a virus that subsequently left him weak for an extended period of time. In his note he wrote:

> Among the things I learned was that joy and suffering were two very separate things, not opposites, not even on the same axis.

May we all learn this lesson and find joy following Christ.

Have you ever experienced joy in the midst of a struggle?

Consider: Nehemiah 8:10; John 15:10-12

Prayer for the Week – Puritan Prayer

> *Lord, high and holy, meek and lowly, You have brought*
> *me to the valley of vision where I live in the depths but*
> *see You in the heights; hemmed in by mountains of sin I*
> *behold Your glory. Let me learn by paradox that the way*
> *down is the way up, that to be low is to be high, that*
> *the broken heart is the healed heart, that the contrite*
> *spirit is the rejoicing spirit, that the repenting soul is the*
> *victorious soul, that to have nothing is to possess all,*
> *that to bear the cross is to wear the crown, that to give*
> *is to receive, that the valley is the place of vision. Lord,*
> *in the daytime stars can be seen from the deepest wells,*
> *and the deeper the wells the brighter Your stars shine;*
> *let me find Your light in my darkness, Your life in my*
> *death, Your joy in my sorrow, Your grace in my sin, Your*
> *riches in my poverty, Your glory in my valley.*

---

[1] David Brooks, "What Suffering Does," *New York Times*, April 7, 2014

[2] See Keller for more on this, Timothy Keller, *Walking with God Through Pain and Suffering*. (Dutton, 2013), p. 28-30.

[3] The contrast between joy and happiness can be confusing because not everyone uses these terms in the same way. Also, the words have evolved in their meaning over time. The ancient Greek philosophers (e.g., Aristotle, etc.) translated the term *eudaimonia* as "human flourishing" or the "highest human good" – i.e., in a way much closer

to what I am arguing is *joy*. Meanwhile, the Greek word for joy (*chara*) is often understood to be part of the supernatural gifts brought by the Holy Spirit. I do not want to dismiss that use!, even as I recognize that today, joy is often seen as a sense of peace and wellbeing that grows out of right living.

[4] The Hebrew word for holiness comes from the root for heavy. Joy does not oppose happiness in the sense of being somber versus laughing; however joy is the opposite of happiness in this sense: happiness is light and joy is weighty.

HELP

Sometimes accepting help is harder than offering it.
— STAR WARS: THE CLONE WARS —

*Pride slays thanksgiving, but a humble mind
is the soil out of which thanks naturally grows.
A proud man is seldom a grateful man,
for he never thinks he gets as much as he deserves.*

— HENRY WARD BEECHER —

One of the last things I say to those I'm visiting in the hospital is, "You realize that you're going to need to accept help going forward, don't you?" Most of the time their reply goes something like this:

> "Yeah, well, uh… that's a problem. I'm not very good at accepting help. I like to give it instead. I like to be the one who helps, not the one who is helped."

I'm often tempted to reply, "Of course you do. There is a word for this. It's called *pride*."

When we are young, Christmas is about the gifts we receive, not the ones we give. But at some point that changes. We prefer to give rather than to get. Likewise, when we are young we appreciate all the help we can get, but at some point receiving from others feels problematic. We sense that we are accruing a debt or being a burden. We want to be the strong, capable, healthy helper, not the sick, wounded, struggling one.

Consequently, when we are struggling we hide so no one sees us. In fact, when we are weak we'd rather go without than let others know we need help. We also generally act as if we are doing better than we are.

As I noted above, there is a word for all of this: *pride*, and pride lies at the root of most of our sin.

According to God, we are supposed to help each other. That is his plan and expectation. It means we must learn to give and receive.

And by the way, allowing others to serve you is often an act of service itself.

Who could you bless by ASKING for help this week?

Consider: John 13:2-8; Ruth 1:16-18

Prayer for the Week – Puritan Prayer

> *Lord, high and holy, meek and lowly, You have brought me to the valley of vision where I live in the depths but see You in the heights; hemmed in by mountains of sin I behold Your glory. Let me learn by paradox that the way down is the way up, that to be low is to be high, that the broken heart is the healed heart, that the contrite spirit is the rejoicing spirit, that the repenting soul is the victorious soul, that to have nothing is to possess all, that to bear the cross is to wear the crown, that to give is to receive, that the valley is the place of vision. Lord, in the daytime stars can be seen from the deepest wells, and the deeper the wells the brighter Your stars shine; let me find Your light in my darkness, Your life in my death, Your joy in my sorrow, Your grace in my sin, Your riches in my poverty, Your glory in my valley.*

HELPLESS

Even though I walk through the darkest valley,
I will fear no evil, for you are with me;
your rod and your staff, they comfort me

— KING DAVID —

The Lord's mercy often rides to the door of our heart
upon the black horse of affliction.

— CHARLES H. SPURGEON —

In an odd way, being helpless was wonderful. I've never felt closer to God. For once I knew that He was in total control and there was nothing I could do to mess that up!

However, as I started to recover, it felt as if God's presence receded. For a while I fought this, asking people to pray that I could hold on to the blessing of his immediacy even as I healed.

Here was a journal entry from May 16th:

> As I regain skills, I am stepping back into the driver's seat. This is not a good thing. I've enjoyed a sweet dependence on Christ over the last few weeks. I feel that slipping away. I don't think it must, and I'm

doing my best to stop it. But it's becoming clear that the challenge of regaining my balance is nothing compared to the challenged of abiding in Christ with the kind of utter dependence I've had over the last few weeks.

After a while, I chose to accept that this was the way it was going to be.

In 2 Cor. 12:9-10. Paul writes:

> But he said to me, "My grace is sufficient for you, for my power is made perfect in weakness." Therefore I will boast all the more gladly about my weaknesses, so that Christ's power may rest on me. That is why, for Christ's sake, I delight in weaknesses, in insults, in hardships, in persecutions, in difficulties. For when I am weak, then I am strong.

Perhaps I will learn how to stay in the place of weakness even when I'm strong. At this moment I do not know how to do that. And rather than stew over that, I am choosing to note – and marvel – that when I needed His care the most, He was there in the biggest way.

When have you felt God's strength supporting your weakness?

Consider: Isaiah 41:9-10; 2 Corinthians 12:9-10

Prayer for the Week – Puritan Prayer

> *Lord, high and holy, meek and lowly, You have brought me to the valley of vision where I live in the depths but see You in the heights; hemmed in by mountains of sin I behold Your glory. Let me learn by paradox that the way down is the way up, that to be low is to be high, that the broken heart is the healed heart, that the contrite spirit is the rejoicing spirit, that the repenting soul is the victorious soul, that to have nothing is to possess all, that to bear the cross is to wear the crown, that to give is to receive, that the valley is the place of vision. Lord, in the daytime stars can be seen from the deepest wells, and the deeper the wells the brighter Your stars shine; let me find Your light in my darkness, Your life in my death, Your joy in my sorrow, Your grace in my sin, Your riches in my poverty, Your glory in my valley.*

JUSTICE

For children are innocent and love justice,
while most of us are wicked and naturally prefer mercy.

— G.K. CHESTERTON —

I love the Lord, for he heard my voice;
he heard my cry for mercy. Because he turned his ear to me,
I will call on him as long as I live.

— PSALM 116:1-2 —

In my April 25th blog entry – one week after my stroke – I tried to address some of the questions people were asking me. Included in that list was this one: "Be honest, are you discouraged? You have to be asking yourself, 'why me?'"

Here was my response:

Medically speaking, I'd sure like an answer to the "why me?" question, because I'd like to ensure it doesn't happen again. But in terms of thinking that God has let me down, it doesn't feel that way at all. In so many respects, this has been a sweet time. It's confirmed the love of my wonderful wife, we've been able to watch our boys step up and act like men, and the stroke has brought greater dependence and intimacy with Christ. As I overheard Sheri say on the phone the other day, "This event has confirmed our faith, not shaken it."

There is a long path ahead of me. I'm sure dark moments lie ahead. Perhaps I will grow discouraged. But I'm not discouraged now. God is good.

Six months later I'd like to add to my answer. I want to more emphatically dismiss some of the underlying assumptions contained in the question.

First, I do not believe that I am entitled to the easy life some people assume I deserve. At least a few think that since I am a pastor – i.e., a holy man! someone who has "given up so much to serve God" – that I deserve good parking, great health and happy children. At the very least, I shouldn't have to suffer as I am.

I do not see things that way at all. In fact, the suggestion that I am holy or special makes me very uneasy. Yes, I have been a Christ-follower for over thirty years. Yes, during most of that time I have been on staff with a church. And yes I try hard to do the right thing. But, I am not a "holy man," nor do I deserve a level of privileged-care not open to others. I am a sinner who is fortunate that God would have me. And the longer I walk with Christ the clearer that becomes for me. I am not doing God any great favors by trying to use the gifts he has given me to pastor a church. I owe him; he does not owe me.

Secondly, I have no interest in justice from God. As a sinful human, getting what I deserve is a scary thought. I want mercy instead. I also want grace – i.e., being blessed in ways I do not deserve.

I've not struggled with the "Why me?" question concerning the stroke. Quite the contrary, for several years I've wondered "Why *not* me?" Why is my life so easy?" And to be honest, it's felt a bit like I've been missing out.

> Consider it pure joy, my brothers and sisters, whenever you face trials of many kinds, because you know that the testing of your faith produces perseverance. Perseverance must finish its work so that you may be mature and complete, not lacking anything. (James 1:2f)

Where are you seeking justice around you?

Consider: Micah 6:8; Psalm 73

Prayer for the Week – Puritan Prayer

> *Lord, high and holy, meek and lowly, You have brought me to the valley of vision where I live in the depths but see You in the heights; hemmed in by mountains of sin I behold Your glory. Let me learn by paradox that the way down is the way up, that to be low is to be high, that the broken heart is the healed heart, that the contrite spirit is the rejoicing spirit, that the repenting soul is the victorious soul, that to have nothing is to possess all, that to bear the cross is to wear the crown, that to give is to receive, that the valley is the place of vision. Lord, in the daytime stars can be seen from the deepest wells, and the deeper the wells the brighter Your stars shine; let me find Your light in my darkness, Your life in my death, Your joy in my sorrow, Your grace in my sin, Your riches in my poverty, Your glory in my valley.*

LIMITATIONS

Love does not grow more quickly because we are in a hurry.
— SKYE JETHANI —

God never hurries. There are no deadlines against which he must work… To know this is to quiet our spirits and relax our nerves.
— A.W. TOZER —

A number of years ago, Pastor John Ortberg asked Dallas Willard – a professor of philosophy at USC and the author of several books on spiritual formation – for advice. John described his own life, listed both the many demands he was juggling and the troubled state of his soul, and then asked, "What should I do?"

There was a long pause, and then Willard said, "You must ruthlessly eliminate hurry from your life."

There was another long pause, after which Ortberg said, somewhat impatiently, "Okay, I've written that one down. What else?"

Another long pause, "There is nothing else," he said. "You must ruthlessly eliminate hurry from your life."

That was years ago. Since then Ortberg has concluded that both his life and the well-being of the people he pastors depends on his following Willard's prescription, for "hurry is the great enemy of spiritual life in our day. Hurry destroys souls. As Carl Jung wrote, 'Hurry is not of the devil; hurry is the devil.'"[1]

Jesus never rushed. He never hurried. Even when his friend Lazarus was dying, he did not race to be with him. This likely grated on at least some of his followers; after all, this unhurried pace drives some of us mad yet today.

One of the blessings of my stroke was forced downtime. Given my limitations – especially my inability to read – there was little I could do other than be. I could pray and reflect – and I do not want to disparage those in any way! – but to employ the idioms of the day:

I could not "make things happen."

I could not "move the needle."

I could not "seize the day."

There was little I could do. I had to just "be."

For those intoxicated with *doing*, *being* can be quite unsettling.

I didn't like it much, but I did learn a few things.

- A frantic, frenetic existence is not a mark of depth

or importance. It certainly isn't a mark of godliness. Quite the opposite, it shows a grasp for control, which suggests self-importance and weak faith.

- Part of what it means to be human is to accept limitations. We cannot be everywhere. We cannot do everything. Jesus accepted these limitations at the time of the incarnation. And he did so on our behalf.

- Rather than trying to do everything, we are invited to surrender our time, our work and our lives to our heavenly Father who is without limitation.

What is adding to the hurriedness of your life? Would it grow or weaken your faith to remove most of these things from your schedule? Invite the One who never hurries to give you his wisdom and perspective.

Where does your schedule make room for God?

Consider: Psalm 1; Luke 5:16

Prayer for the Week – St. Francis

> *Lord, make me an instrument of your peace. Where there is hatred, let me sow love. Where there is injury, pardon. Where there is doubt, faith. Where there is despair, hope. Where there is darkness, light. Where there is sadness, joy. O Divine Master, grant that I may not so much seek to be consoled as to console, not so much to be understood as to understand, not so much to be loved, as to love; for it is in giving that we receive, it is in pardoning that we are pardoned, it is in dying that we awake to eternal life.*

---

[1] John Ortberg, "Ruthlessly Eliminate Hurry," *Christianity Today*, 2002, www.christianitytoday.com/le/2002/july-online-only/cln20704.html?start=2.

NEED

The world says: "You have needs – satisfy them.
You have as much right as the rich and the mighty.
Don't hesitate to satisfy your needs; indeed, expand your
needs and demand more." This is the worldly doctrine
of today. And they believe that this is freedom.
The result for the rich is isolation and suicide,
for the poor, envy and murder.

— FYODOR DOSTOYEVSKY, *THE BROTHERS KARAMAZOV* —

Jesus Christ is all you need, but you will never know it
until He is all you have. And when He is all you have,
then you will know that He is all you need.

— RON DUNN —

————————————————

According to Abraham Maslow, the onetime president of
the American Psychological Association and the architect
for what is now called Maslow's Hierarchy of Needs (see
diagram), we all have categories of needs. Our physiological
needs (food, air, water, etc.) are the most urgent. If they are
met then we are free to focus on our safety needs. Once they
are met we move on (and up) to love and self-esteem needs.
If we excel at this level (per Maslow's definition) then we are
among the few who can focus on self-actualization.

Jesus describes things differently. In fact, his teaching that "the first will be last," "the greatest will serve" and the "most loving will sacrifice their life for another," all suggest that he'd think Maslow has at least a few things upside down.

I'm not arguing that we do not have real needs. We do. Indeed, though we are made in the image of a self-sufficient God, we are dependent creatures who rely on God for life, breath, food and more. What I am arguing is that the way up is down; and this requires us to differentiate between needs and wants.

The Way Up is Down: No one started higher or descended lower than Jesus. Paul makes this profoundly clear when he weaves what is perhaps the oldest hymn on record into the second chapter of his letter to the church in Philippi. There we read:

"… have the same mindset as Christ Jesus:

Who, being in very nature God,
   did not consider equality with God
something to be used to his own advantage;
rather, he made himself nothing
   by taking the very nature of a servant,
   being made in human likeness.
And being found in appearance as a man,
   he humbled himself
   by becoming obedient to death—
     even death on a cross!"

By all accounts, Jesus climbed down the ladder of success, making do with less and less in order to serve others.

Wants versus needs: We live in a culture where smart people want to convince us that we need things we do not. They are incessantly promoting newer, faster and bigger, and trying to persuade us that without their gizmo we are missing out. But the truth is: these products seldom bring the benefits their promoters promise; and we need a lot less than we think. (Indeed, the longer I live the less I want.)

If you do not learn to tell a real need from a want-masquerading-as-a-need, you will never find peace and rest, because you can never get enough – or buy enough – wants to satisfy your soul. The way forward is to learn to differentiate a want from a need, and to learn to want less.

This takes time, effort and reflection. But it is possible, and we can do no better than to begin our reflection on Christ's words from the Sermon on the Mount:

> So do not worry, saying, 'What shall we eat?' or 'What shall we drink?' or 'What shall we wear?' For the pagans run after all these things, and your heavenly Father knows that you need them. But seek first his kingdom and his righteousness, and all these things will be given to you as well.

What are your top ten needs today?

Consider: Matthew 6:28-34; Philippians 2:2-13

Prayer for the Week – St. Francis

> *Lord, make me an instrument of your peace. Where there is hatred, let me sow love. Where there is injury, pardon. Where there is doubt, faith. Where there is despair, hope. Where there is darkness, light. Where there is sadness, joy. O Divine Master, grant that I may not so much seek to be consoled as to console, not so much to be understood as to understand, not so much to be loved, as to love; for it is in giving that we receive, it is in pardoning that we are pardoned, it is in dying that we awake to eternal life.*

PAIN

Pain insists upon being attended to. God whispers to us in our pleasures, speaks in our consciences, but shouts in our pains. It is his megaphone to rouse a deaf world.

— C.S. LEWIS —

One of the side effects of my stroke is that I am not able to feel temperatures on the right side of my body. My doctors say that my ability to tell hot from cold might return over time. Perhaps it will. Over the last few months, cold has started to hurt – not terribly, but enough to make picking up a glass of ice-water with my right hand uncomfortable. Meanwhile, hot doesn't register at all.

Lest you think this might have some advantages, think again. It turns out that feeling in general and pain in particular is a real blessing.

I first realized this when I was shaving a couple months after the stroke. I rinsed the shaving cream off of my right hand without thinking anything about it, then put my left hand under the water to do the same only to realize that it was scalding hot.

I could have seriously burned myself without realizing it.

I have a friend who has a similar condition, also because of a stroke. Several years ago he burned himself quite severely with a glue gun. He knew it was hot, but didn't realize it was touching his leg until someone pointed it out.

We do not like pain, but as it turns out, it's quite helpful.[1] In fact, it's so helpful that some doctors delay relieving pain because it helps them understand exactly what is going on. As it turns out, physical pain is important to our well-being.

Emotional pain is necessary as well. Over the years I've met with people who complain of being depressed. Sometimes the reason they feel blue is rather mysterious. But other times it is not. After they describe what has been going on in their life I say, "You should be depressed. I'm depressed just hearing your story. It's right for you to be hurting right now. It means your heart is working. I'd be more concerned for you if you were not depressed."

We do not like pain – of any type – but it's an important early warning system that things are wrong and we need to take action.

Pain is another of the many gifts from God.

When has pain in your life helped you address a deeper issue?

Consider: Psalm 30:5; 1 Peter 4:12-13

Prayer for the Week – St. Francis

> *Lord, make me an instrument of your peace. Where there is hatred, let me sow love. Where there is injury, pardon. Where there is doubt, faith. Where there is despair, hope. Where there is darkness, light. Where there is sadness, joy. O Divine Master, grant that I may not so much seek to be consoled as to console, not so much to be understood as to understand, not so much to be loved, as to love; for it is in giving that we receive, it is in pardoning that we are pardoned, it is in dying that we awake to eternal life.*

---

[1] This is not a celebration of pain for pain's sake. That's masochism. We are called to self-denial, but only for a greater reward.

REGRET

Suffering has been stronger than all other teaching,
and has taught me to understand what your heart used to be.
I have been bent and broken, but - I hope - into a better shape.
— CHARLES DICKENS —

We must learn to regard people less in the light of what they
do or omit to do, and more in the light of what they suffer.
— DIETRICH BONHOEFFER —

Near the end of his life, John Stott was asked, "What is your biggest regret?"

As you may know, Dr. Stott was an enormously accomplished man – the author of numerous important and best-selling books, Chaplain to the Queen and trusted advisor and confidant to many of the 20th century's most influential Christian leaders (e.g., Billy Graham, Rick Warren, etc.). Stott was also a principal architect behind the Lausanne Movement and the founder of both the Langham Trust and the London Institute of Contemporary Christianity.

His prominence was such that I think *New York Times* columnist David Brooks referred to Stott as "the Protestant Pope," and I agree.

And yet on top of all of this, Stott was one of the most humble and Christ-like people I ever spent time with. He was kind. He lived simply and he went out of his way to help others.

So when I heard him asked, "What do you regret?" I was very curious about how he'd answer the question. I'd heard that in the Byzantine politics of the Anglican Church he had been blocked from moving up their ranks – and that at one time that had bothered him. But I couldn't imagine it would be his chief regret.

So how did he answer? Without pausing for more than a second, Stott said, "My chief regret is that I have never suffered for my Lord, who suffered so much for me."

It seems to me that this calls for a few moments of reflection: we invest lots of time trying to avoid suffering of any type, while the chief regret of one of the godliest people of the 20th century is that he didn't suffer enough.

How do you want your friends and family to think about you?

Consider: Romans 13:8-10; Ephesians 5:15-17

Prayer for the Week – St. Francis

> *Lord, make me an instrument of your peace. Where there is hatred, let me sow love. Where there is injury, pardon. Where there is doubt, faith. Where there is despair, hope. Where there is darkness, light. Where there is sadness, joy. O Divine Master, grant that I may not so much seek to be consoled as to console, not so much to be understood as to understand, not so much to be loved, as to love; for it is in giving that we receive, it is in pardoning that we are pardoned, it is in dying that we awake to eternal life.*

RESILIENCE

It always seems impossible until it's done.

— NELSON MANDELA —

Not that I have already obtained all this, or have already arrived at my goal, but I press on to take hold of that for which Christ Jesus took hold of me. Brothers and sisters, I do not consider myself yet to have taken hold of it. But one thing I do: Forgetting what is behind and straining toward what is ahead, I press on toward the goal to win the prize for which God has called me heavenward in Christ Jesus.

— THE APOSTLE PAUL —

On May 8th I wrote the following:[1]

> In *The Silver Chair,* one of C.S. Lewis' Chronicles of Narnia, Jill is reduced to tears. She goes to her room and cries for a while and then, in vintage fashion, Lewis describes not only Jill's dilemma but ours as well, "Crying is all right in its way while it lasts. But you have to stop sooner or later, and then you still have to decide what to do."
>
> I wasn't reduced to tears today, but I got very frustrated and started feeling very sorry for myself. At one point during an "aerobics class" (that I was engaged in from my wheel chair) I was overwhelmed

by how much I had lost. Let me be clear. Through no merit of my own, I enjoy more physical abilities than ninety percent of the people in this rehab facility. And I'm seeing great progress – every day I'm getting stronger and better. But during the aerobics class I was struck by how much ability I had lost and I wanted to quit. I might have, but I remembered Lewis's line and I thought: "So what if I quit this class and go off and sulk? What does that accomplish? At some point I have to figure out what I am going to do. At some point I have to face these challenges that lie ahead and work through them."

I frequently quote the Apostle Paul's admonition to "Press on." It comes from Philippians 3:12-21 where we are told to "press on toward the goal to win the prize for which God has called me heavenward in Christ Jesus." It's when we don't want to press on that it's most important that we do. The changes that we most need to see in our lives can only be accomplished through the grace of God. We cannot change our heart in the right way on our own. But we are not passive in the process. Sometimes growth comes easily. But most of the time it requires a great deal of tenacity.

"Crying is all right in its way while it lasts. But you have to stop sooner or later, and then you still have to decide what to do." Let's decide that we want to become more like Jesus.

How does God help us to "press on" in difficulty?

Consider: Philippians 3:15-21; Psalm 30

Prayer for the Week – St. Francis

> *Lord, make me an instrument of your peace. Where there is hatred, let me sow love. Where there is injury, pardon. Where there is doubt, faith. Where there is despair, hope. Where there is darkness, light. Where there is sadness, joy. O Divine Master, grant that I may not so much seek to be consoled as to console, not so much to be understood as to understand, not so much to be loved, as to love; for it is in giving that we receive, it is in pardoning that we are pardoned, it is in dying that we awake to eternal life.*

---

[1] To say I "wrote" is misleading. For the first few months I had trouble seeing and I lacked the coordination to type, so I dictated these entries.

RISK

He is no fool who gives what he cannot keep to gain
that which he cannot lose.

— JIM ELLIOT —

Not so long ago it was common for parents to tell their children to be brave. Now they tell them to "be careful." The assumption is that we must avoid all risk.

We have been duped into thinking that we are always better off safe.

And yet, the Bible suggests that risk is often right. Not the imprudent risk we embrace in the pursuit of glory, nor the needless danger we submit others to for our gain, but the prudent risk we embrace when we step forward in faith in God.[1]

Risk is right. Courage and bravery are part of the good life. Besides, sometimes the most dangerous thing we can do is avoid risk.

Consider the spies of Numbers 13. Shortly after escaping from Egypt, Moses directed twelve men to scout out the Promised Land and then report back to the people. This is what follows:

> They came back to Moses and Aaron and the whole
> Israelite community at Kadesh in the Desert of
> Paran. There they reported to them and to the whole
> assembly and showed them the fruit of the land. They
> gave Moses this account: "We went into the land to
> which you sent us, and it does flow with milk and
> honey! Here is its fruit. But the people who live there
> are powerful, and the cities are fortified and very
> large. We even saw descendants of Anak there. The
> Amalekites live in the Negev; the Hittites, Jebusites
> and Amorites live in the hill country; and the
> Canaanites live near the sea and along the Jordan."

> Then Caleb silenced the people before Moses and
> said, "We should go up and take possession of the
> land, for we can certainly do it."

> But the men who had gone up with him said, "We
> can't attack those people; they are stronger than
> we are." And they spread among the Israelites a bad
> report about the land they had explored. They said,
> "The land we explored devours those living in it. All
> the people we saw there are of great size. We saw the
> Nephilim there (the descendants of Anak come from
> the Nephilim). We seemed like grasshoppers in our
> own eyes, and we looked the same to them."

God said, "Go." But the spies said, "No." And so the people decided to "play it safe." The result? They spent the next forty years doing laps in the Sinai Desert while waiting to die.

One of the things my stroke taught me is that I need to take more risks. I (we) often settle for less than God wants (or expects) for lack of a little risk. Besides, life is short and the opportunity to make a difference is not open-ended. It is now.

My stroke showed me ways in which I've become soft. Living in a culture where everyone wears bike helmets, fastens seat-belts and puts on life-preservers – all in an effort to "be safe" – has led me to avoid risk. I seldom ask: safe for what? To what end? Or, what would faith and courage look like at this moment?

Thomas Aquinas noted that "if the primary aim of a captain were to preserve his ship, he would keep it in port forever."

Our goal is not to be safe. Our goal is to please God.
We need to run some risks, take some chances and live dangerously for the kingdom of God.

When did you last choose bravery over safety?

Consider: 1 Samuel 17:45-47; Esther 4:12-16

Prayer for the Week – St. Francis

> *Lord, make me an instrument of your peace. Where
> there is hatred, let me sow love. Where there is injury,
> pardon. Where there is doubt, faith. Where there is
> despair, hope. Where there is darkness, light. Where
> there is sadness, joy. O Divine Master, grant that I may
> not so much seek to be consoled as to console, not so
> much to be understood as to understand, not so much
> to be loved, as to love; for it is in giving that we receive,
> it is in pardoning that we are pardoned, it is in dying
> that we awake to eternal life.*

---

[1] Today many associate risk-taking with things like sky-diving or bungee jumping – events which serve no purpose except the thrill of the act. This is not the kind of risk-taking I am advocating. Rather, it is the courageous acts that flow out of a life of faith in God.

SELF-SUFFICIENCY

When pride comes, then comes disgrace,
but with humility comes wisdom.
— PROVERBS 11:2 —

Don't be so naive and self-confident. You're not exempt. You
could fall flat on your face as easily as anyone else. Forget
about self-confidence; it's useless. Cultivate God-confidence.
— THE APOSTLE PAUL —

Failure is easier to handle than success.

By this I do not mean that it's easier to fail than to succeed. That's usually true but hardly a headline. What I am arguing is that those who experience a steady diet of small failures often avoid the catastrophic events that some experience. There is nothing like striking out a few times to keep your ego in check.

Humility especially helps on the spiritual front. As C.S. Lewis noted in *Mere Christianity*:

> A proud man is always looking down on things and people; and, of course, as long as you are looking down, you cannot see something that is above you.

I've witnessed a few truly spectacular falls – failures so complete that the elevator dropped from the penthouse to the parking garage without stopping once. In every case these were people who read their own press-releases. In some cases, I suspect, they even handed them out.

They were not simply brazen. They were brazenly brazen.

Why can so few people handle success? Why do so many with power become blind to the way it changes them for the worst? In many cases it's because we become proud, and as Solomon notes, after pride shows up you can count on a fall.

But something else is in play. My recent face-plant leaves me thinking that self-sufficiency is, at best, a temporary condition.

On the night of my stroke I was helpless. In fact, after getting out of bed to go to the bathroom , I discovered that I couldn't even crawl there. I had to be picked up and set back in bed. I couldn't get there on my own. I recall thinking two things at that moment. First, something profound had just happened for the first time. I'd just experienced a Cat's-in-the-Cradle moment.[1] I'd picked up my boys before – I'd held them. But they had never held me. At that moment I remember being amazed at how unexpected this was. I never saw it coming.

Secondly, I remember marveling at how utterly dependent I had become. For the first time in years I realized that I was not only unable to work my way out of the hole I was in, I wasn't even able to make any contribution. I couldn't "leverage my network," "call in favors," or "throw my money" at the problem. If others didn't come through for me there was nothing I could do about it.

Independence is a myth. Self-control is a temporary illusion.

Broken people get this. Successful ones often forget it.

Who could you thank for being there with you through life?

Consider: Proverbs 11:1-7; 1 Corinthians 10:11-13

Prayer for the Week – St. Augustine

> *Breathe in me, O Holy Spirit, that my thoughts may all be holy. Act in me, O Holy Spirit, that my work, too, may be holy. Draw my heart, O Holy Spirit, that I may love only what is holy. Strengthen me, O Holy Spirit, that I may defend all that is holy. Guard me, O Holy Spirit, that I myself may always be holy.*

---

[1] This is an allusion to a 1974 folk rock song by Harry Chapin that tells the story of a father who is too busy to spend time with his son and the son who promises to grow up just like him. In the end the father – who is now much older – wants to spend time with his son but his son is now too busy. I use it here to allude to the idea that I was stepping down and my boys were stepping into the lead role, and doing so much sooner than I would have ever imagined.

SIN

There but for the grace of God go I.

— JOHN BRADFORD —

The quote listed above is commonly attributed to John Bradford, a 16th century preacher who was martyred for his faith. According to tradition, whenever Bradford saw someone being led to the gallows, he would announce, "There, but for the grace of God, go I."

In other words, Bradford believed that had God not redirected his life, he would have followed the same path as the man being led to the gallows.

One of the blessings my recent struggles provided me was a glimpse of my own weakness – an awareness of how easily I could end up in deep trouble. In particular it showed me how quickly I could end up addicted to some kind of pain-numbing substance.

In the first days after my stroke I had an unusually painful headache and none of the standard medications was able to provide me with any relief. My neurologist kept trying different drugs until one day he found one that worked: Percocet. I loved it. And apparently I started asking

for it more and more often, which eventually led to this
conversation with the neurologist:

Dr.:   I see you really liked the Percocet.

Me: Yes! It works. It's wonderful. It takes away most of
the pain.

Dr.:   Well I'm taking you off it.

Me: What? Why? How could you?

Dr.:   Don't worry. I'm approving you for Narcogin
instead.

Me: Narcogin? You're putting me on a narcotic?
You'd rather give me a narcotic than Percocet?

Dr.:   I'm more concerned about the Percocet than a
narcotic.

After a few moments of reflection I announced that I was
unwilling to take either.

Why did I take such a hard line? There were two reasons.
First, because I know a number of people who are still
struggling – years later – to break addictions to prescription
pain killers. And most of them developed their addictions
while in the hospital. I didn't want to start down that path.

Second, because suddenly the pain killer reminded me of
sin. And one of the things we know about sin is that every
sin makes the next one easier.

Please understand me; I am not suggesting that taking pain killers is wrong. It is just that I suddenly realized how weak I was in the face of the pain I was experiencing, and it occurred to me that if I took another step down this path I would not be able to stop.

Sin is nothing other than defective good. Consequently it can never ultimately satisfy us; it just draws us deeper and deeper down the wrong path. I was just clear-headed enough to know that if I barely had the strength to say "no" to Narcogin now, I was pretty likely to be demanding it every few hours once I started.

And desperate people do desperate things. I needed to take a stand while I still could.

Perhaps Narcogin would have been an easy habit to break. I'm not in the habit of overruling neurologists when it comes to pain meds. But I've dealt with sin before. I know its relentless pull.

Every sin makes the next one easier. Say "no" today.

What past struggle has God helped you overcome?
Praise Him.

Consider: Romans 7:14-25; Romans 6:23

Prayer for the Week – St. Augustine

> *Breathe in me, O Holy Spirit, that my thoughts may all be holy. Act in me, O Holy Spirit, that my work, too, may be holy. Draw my heart, O Holy Spirit, that I may love only what is holy. Strengthen me, O Holy Spirit, that I may defend all that is holy. Guard me, O Holy Spirit, that I myself may always be holy.*

SUFFER

Maybe the truly handicapped people are the ones that don't need God as much.

— JONI EARECKSON TADA —

We plan for happiness, but we're formed by suffering.

— DAVID BROOKS —

Ask someone when they grew the most and they'll talk about a season of turmoil, change and loss. It's often when we feel scared and helpless that we rely on God and move forward. We'd seldom choose the events that help us grow. Indeed, we often fear them. But after we survive them we look back on them with thanks. Our suffering changed us. It made us better.

I know people who claim that getting cancer was the best thing to happen to them, or that being fired was a huge blessing in disguise. I'm not quite able to unconditionally celebrate my stroke. I'm glad for the insights and texture it has added to my life, but the tuition payment was (is!) pretty high.[1]

Having said that, it's clear that the stroke has been a net positive experience.

I like comfort, but I grow most when things are hardest.

When has God been able to be your strength?

Consider: 2 Corinthians 12:8-10; Psalm 40

Prayer for the Week – St. Augustine

Breathe in me, O Holy Spirit, that my thoughts may all be holy. Act in me, O Holy Spirit, that my work, too, may be holy. Draw my heart, O Holy Spirit, that I may love only what is holy. Strengthen me, O Holy Spirit, that I may defend all that is holy. Guard me, O Holy Spirit, that I myself may always be holy.

---

[1] One of the other reasons I hesitate to say something like, "I am so glad this happened and I'd sign up for it again," is that it placed huge demands on my family, especially Sheri. And since I am still not driving, the demands are ongoing. No one is complaining about any of this, but it would seem wrong for me to sign us all up for my stroke without acknowledging that my stroke impacted my entire family, and I do not want to put them through that again.

SURRENDER

He must increase; I must decrease.

— JOHN THE BAPTIST —

If we grow most during seasons of upheaval, must we wait for painful trials in order to draw closer to God? No. There is always another option, though when things are going well we are less inclined to look for God's help; the person of faith may *choose* to yield control of their life to God.[1]

This yielding – which some call surrender – is hard. It's easier to operate under our own power. Furthermore, it's not a one-time event. We must keep yielding, day-by-day, hour-by-hour. Sometimes it's a moment-by-moment decision.

How do we surrender? I find it hard to answer that question. My attempts to do so all sound quite mystical. But here are some thoughts that may help:

- Rick Warren says that you can know that you have surrendered to God when: you rely on God to work things out instead of trying to manipulate others, force your agenda and control the situation. You let go and let God work. You don't have to always be in charge. *Instead of trying harder, you trust more.*

- My experience is that if I want to gain greater control in an area – e.g., I want to learn to trust more or not be so angry – the path forward often comes through surrender in other areas, like fasting. Dallas Willard defines spiritual disciplines as activities within our power that enable us to accomplish what we cannot do by direct effort in other areas. We are then able to take ground because of God's power working within us.

- Surrendered hearts are not self-serving; nor are they protective of ego. A spiritually mature person is almost impossible to insult, because their pride is so fully in check.

- The most difficult thing for most people to surrender is their money. Many think, "I want to live for God but I also want to live comfortably and save for retirement." The Bible applauds planning (i.e., saving for the future) but it also warns about the ability of money to corrupt. The security and power money brings typically competes with God.

- The supreme example of surrender is Jesus. The night before his crucifixion Jesus surrendered himself to God's plan. He prayed, *"Abba,* Father, everything is possible for you. Take this cup from me. Yet not what I will, but what you will."

- Genuine surrender says, "Father, if this problem, pain, sickness or circumstance is needed to fulfill your purpose and glory in my life or in another's life, please don't take it away!"

Is there an area of life you find the hardest to entrust to God?

Consider: Matthew 11:28-30; Luke 22:39-46

Prayer for the Week – St. Augustine

> *Breathe in me, O Holy Spirit, that my thoughts may all be holy. Act in me, O Holy Spirit, that my work, too, may be holy. Draw my heart, O Holy Spirit, that I may love only what is holy. Strengthen me, O Holy Spirit, that I may defend all that is holy. Guard me, O Holy Spirit, that I myself may always be holy.*

---

[1] Writing about this, Skye Jethani notes, "Repeatedly in Scripture we see that God often does his most creative work by dislocating his people – by calling them to leave the familiar circumstances in which they feel in control. Theologians call it "creative dislocation." By willingly accepting foreign circumstances, the illusion of control is disrupted and we open ourselves to the creative work of God and greater intimacy with him."

TRIALS

Our vision is so limited we can hardly imagine a love that does not show itself in protection from suffering.... The love of God did not protect His own Son.... He will not necessarily protect us - not from anything it takes to make us like His Son. A lot of hammering and chiseling and purifying by fire will have to go into the process.

— ELIZABETH ELLIOT —

When pain and suffering come upon us, we finally see not only that we are not in control of our lives, but that we never were.

— TIM KELLER —

The series, *Broken,* was about trials – all five books and all six sermons – so I have few unexpressed thoughts on the topic. But something did strike me the other morning. It's not a new thought but it hit me with more force than it ever has before. One of the advantages of a major trial – and consequently, one of the things I now miss – is the clear understanding that we are in a trial and need to look to God for help.

If the problem is big enough, or we are scared enough, we turn to God. If not, we often mistakenly think we can manage on our own.

Perhaps the most dangerous moments in our lives are not when we are about to be thrown to the lions or placed in a fiery furnace – we see those threats for what they are. Instead the most dangerous moments in our lives are the ordinary, vanilla days when we mistakenly think we have everything under control.

God may overturn our apple cart simply so we become better people.

How can you practice trusting dependency on God – all the time?

Consider: 1 Thessalonians 3:1-5; Psalm 52:6-9

Prayer for the Week – St. Augustine

> *Breathe in me, O Holy Spirit, that my thoughts may all be holy. Act in me, O Holy Spirit, that my work, too, may be holy. Draw my heart, O Holy Spirit, that I may love only what is holy. Strengthen me, O Holy Spirit, that I may defend all that is holy. Guard me, O Holy Spirit, that I myself may always be holy.*

TRUTH

Facts do not cease to exist because they are ignored.

— ALDOUS HUXLEY —

My May 14th blog entry read as follows:

> My brain thinks I'm falling to the right, so it is forever throwing me to the left. Therapists strap weights onto my right side and stand me in front of a mirror so that I have clear reference points. But as soon as I let go of the railing I throw myself to the left. It's almost comical. No matter how hard I try to focus on standing up straight – and not throwing myself to the left - I always do. My internal gyroscope is off, consequently it doesn't matter what I see; things feel wrong and what feels right inside me overrides objective reality.

> I'm struck by how many ways this metaphor could be applied. We all have an internal sense of right and wrong with regard to politics, economics, theology, culture and more. But even when someone shows us the plumb-line of truth we don't trust it. Our internal gyroscope overrides the objective reality.

> May we all find True North!

As I review this blog entry nearly six months later, I am thankful that my internal gyroscope has adjusted itself. It's not perfect; consequently I still stumble a bit, especially in the mornings or when I get tired. But I can stand on my own without holding on to a railing. (I'm even able to briefly stand up straight with my eyes closed.) I've made a lot of progress in seven months and have much to be thankful for.

But I am discouraged by the way my experiences translate into other arenas. Our culture is increasingly polarized. We are moving further away from objective standards (e.g., the Bible) in favor of our internal gyroscope. And while that gyroscope feels right, it often is off.

On what do you base your judgments of right or wrong?

Consider: 1 Timothy 3:15-16; Psalm 19:7-10

Prayer for the Week – St. Augustine

> *Breathe in me, O Holy Spirit, that my thoughts may all be holy. Act in me, O Holy Spirit, that my work, too, may be holy. Draw my heart, O Holy Spirit, that I may love only what is holy. Strengthen me, O Holy Spirit, that I may defend all that is holy. Guard me, O Holy Spirit, that I myself may always be holy.*

BIOGRAPHY

Mike Woodruff is the senior pastor of Christ Church, a growing community church with campuses in Lake Forest, Highland Park, and Crossroads in Grayslake IL. In addition to founding *The Ivy Jungle Network* and serving as the President of *Scholar Leaders International,* Mike has worked as both a college minister and management consultant. As an author he has published over two hundred articles for business and ministry publications and edited or contributed to several books. He holds degrees from DePauw University and Trinity Evangelical Divinity School. Mike and his wife Sheri have three sons, Austin, Benjamin and Jason. You can hear his teaching on the radio program, *Pressing On with Mike Woodruff,* weekdays at 3:30 p.m. on AM 1160 (WYLL). Visit the Christ Church website at *www.christchurchil.org* and Mike's blog at *www.mikewoodruff.org* to learn more.

Broken: Preparing for the Day When Life Stops Working and Your Faith Is Tested.

Christ Church is one church in three locations:

Christ Church Crossroads
1350 IL Route 137 Grayslake, IL 60030

Christ Church Highland Park
1713 Green Bay Rd. Highland Park, IL 60035

Christ Church Lake Forest
100 N. Waukegan Rd. Lake Forest, IL 60045

For more information on service times
call **847.234.1001** or visit **www.christchurchil.org**